HIKING
the
SuAsCo Watershed

Exploring
the Woods and Waters
of the
Sudbury, Assabet and
Concord Rivers

Jill Phelps Kern

New England Cartographics
2004
www.necartographics.com

Library of Congress Control # 2004101145
Manufactured in the United States of America
ISBN 1-889787-11-6

Text and photographs by Jill Phelps Kern
Editing and typesetting by Valerie Vaughan

10 9 8 7 6 5 4 3 2 1   10 09 08 07 06 05 04

Attention Hikers!

*** Due to possible changes in trail conditions,
the use of information in this book is at the sole risk of the user.**

***Some trails may cross through or near portions of private land
and may not be open to the public. Please respect the rights of owners.**

---

*Any changes, corrections, comments or suggestions
about the hikes in this book are welcome.
Please send them to the author c/o New England Cartographics.*

Table of Contents

Hike Descriptions

Hike Locations

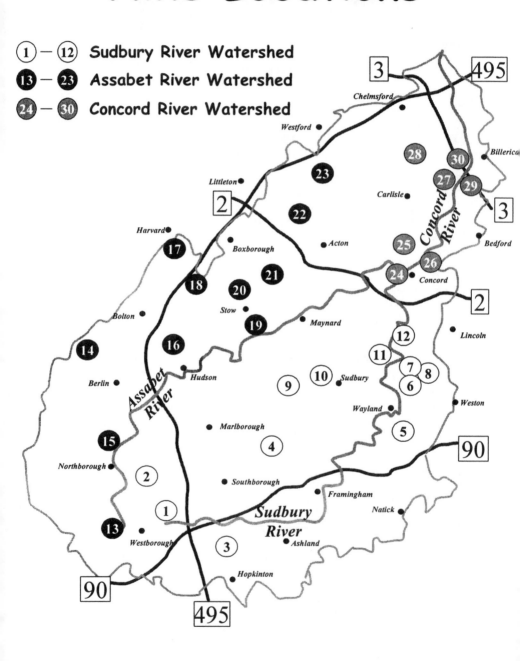

1 — 12 Sudbury River Watershed
13 — 23 Assabet River Watershed
24 — 30 Concord River Watershed

Summary of Suggested Hikes

#	Town	Property	Rating	Length

Sudbury River Watershed

#	Town	Property	Rating	Length
1	Westborough	Walkup and Robinson Memorial	Moderate	3.1 mi
2	Northborough	Cedar Hill	Moderate	2.4 mi
3	Hopkinton	Hopkinton State Park	Challenging (length)	6.6 mi
4	Framingham	Gibbs Mountain / Beebe Pond	Challenging (steep)	3.7 mi
5	Wayland	Hamlen Woods	Moderate	3.0 mi
6	Wayland	Upper Mill Brook	Easy	3.2 mi
7	Wayland	School House Pond / Trout Brook	Moderate	2.0 mi
8	Wayland	Hazel Brook / Weston Town Forest	Moderate	4.0 mi
9	Sudbury	Hop Brook / Memorial Forest	Easy	3.4 mi
10	Sudbury	Gray Reservation	Easy (1 steep section)	1.9 mi
11	Sudbury	Weir Hill / Round Hill	Moderate	2.1 mi
12	Lincoln	Mount Misery / Farrar Pond	Moderate	5.0 mi

Assabet River Watershed

#	Town	Property	Rating	Length
13	Westborough	Headwaters Conservation Area	Moderate	1.7 mi
14	Berlin	Garfield Woods / Forty Caves	Moderate	2.3 mi
15	Northborough	Edmund Hill	Moderate	2.0 mi
16	Hudson	Danforth Falls	Moderate	1.7 mi
17	Harvard	Great Elms / Williams Pond	Moderate	2.5 mi
18	Harvard	Delaney Project	Moderate	4.4 mi
19	Stow	Gardner Hill	Moderate	2.7 mi
20	Stow	Heath Hen Meadow Brook Woodland	Easy	1.4 mi
21	Acton	Heath Hen Meadow	Easy	2.8 mi
22	Acton	Grassy Pond / Nagog Hill	Moderate	3.0 mi
23	Westford	Nashoba Pond	Moderate	1.9 mi

Concord River Watershed

#	Town	Property	Rating	Length
24	Concord	Egg Rock	Easy	2.3 mi
25	Concord	Estabrook Woods	Easy	4.2 mi
26	Concord	Great Meadows Nat'l Wildlife Refuge	Easy	3.1 mi
27	Carlisle	River Meadows	Moderate	4.8 mi
28	Carlisle	Great Brook Farm State Park	Moderate	4.1 mi
29	Bedford	Minnie Reid / Huckins Farm	Easy	3.3 mi
30	Billerica	Vietnam Veterans Park / Ralph Hill	Moderate	2.0 mi

Foreword

Swaths of conservation land, large enough to support wildlife and to provide good, long walks, help to make eastern Massachusetts a wonderful place to live. The patch of Earth that is drained by the Sudbury, Assabet and Concord Rivers resembles in shape the leaf of a swamp white oak tree, with its stem pointing to the northeast. Because this area receives ample precipitation, this watershed is well-veined with streams and supports a lush growth of plants.

This moisture and vegetation pose challenges for hikers, however. In dense woods, it is easy to become disoriented; the undergrowth slows the hiking pace; and water often bars the way. To surmount these obstacles, hikers need trails, footbridges, and reliable maps. Fortunately, we have among us some people whose idea of fun includes building and maintaining good walking trails. There are also organizations which support and coordinate the work of these public-spirited individuals and which have marked out routes that keep hikers from getting lost.

To explore our pockets of wilderness, we have to know where to park our vehicles and find the trailhead. This book takes us to places where the trails await us; it provides the maps and guidance for rambling within the natural beauty of our region. For the great places that aren't easy to find, Jill Phelps Kern's scouting reports give us access, and her infectious enthusiasm alerts us to their riches. Both her guidance and her zeal are expressed with a clarity and compactness that make her work all the more welcome. For years to come, this will surely be the book most likely to be carried by our regions's hikers.

Ron McAdow
Executive Director, Sudbury Valley Trustees

Introduction

What draws us to woods and to water?

Modern commerce circulates on paved highways and roads, through the air, over oceans and lakes, and along major rivers. The machinery of industry requires breadth, smoothness -- and above all, speed. We find balance for this speed along the narrow, bumpy trails of our woodlands; we find respite from its noise in the gurgles and splashes of brooks and streams. These waterways are the arteries and capillaries of our planet, part of the circulatory system that, along with the less visible flows of air in our atmosphere and currents in our seas, helps keep this earth alive.

I love tramping the quiet paths that weave a hidden network away from the pavement that we travel almost unconsciously every day. In the woods my pace slows to the speed of nature – an evolutionary pace, with space to see, hear, smell, feel as a single organism among the billions on our planet. I feel like a clandestine scout padding along behind the scenes, glimpsing the feathering of a nest, the emergence of a mushroom, the mating of snakes, the feeding of a doe, the relentless tiptoeing of a painted turtle.

There's a kind of glee in exploring these trails – invisibly probing the expanses beyond our back yards, finding out how our towns are knit together, discovering how brooks feed ponds, how the ponds release themselves into streams, and the streams merge into rivers. There are no dotted lines along the forest floor, showing where Carlisle and Concord rub shoulders, only the occasional solitary granite stele staking its claim to a corner of a map.

In these woods and along these waterways, every season provides joy and challenge to the hiker – from the mud and bursting new green of spring, the insects and cooling foliage of summer, the colors of autumn segueing into bare branches and re-opened views, to the snowy trails and pristine solitude of winter. Explore throughout the year – with appropriate equipment and supplies – and you'll have the chance to find the unfamiliar or unexpected: blossoms and scents, adult geese shepherding fuzzy youngsters, raccoon tracks in the snow … and more, along the trails of the SuAsCo watershed.

Enjoy!

Jill Phelps Kern

Remnants of former bridge foundation
River Meadows Reservation, Carlisle (Hike # 27)

Watershed Origins

The stone-studded character of the Massachusetts landscape began to take shape between one billion and twelve million years ago as the earth's surface cooled. Mountains the height of the Rockies rose and wore away, their remains mixing with volcanic lava to form a rich soil. Then came the Ice Age, lasting one million years and bringing four successive glaciers, so massive they eventually pressed the landscape downward by hundreds of feet.

The last glacier melted away about 15,000 years ago, having scraped off the soil, scoured the bedrock, and left loose boulders (erratics) scattered far from their origins. Glacial hills (drumlins) and ridges (eskers) remain, formed from glacial debris -- rocks, gravel and sand. Swamps and bogs evolved where chunks of glacial ice melted into ponds, then silted up.

Melt waters left by the retreat of the glaciers in central Massachusetts formed glacial Lake Assabet. Once the weight of the ice was gone, the land rose up again in what geologists call "rebound," much of the water drained away, and glacial Lake Assabet ebbed down into three separate basins. The remnant of the western part is now under the SuAsCo Reservoir, source of the Assabet River. The northern portion survives today as Chauncy Lake and Crane Swamp. The easternmost section became Cedar Swamp, the largest remnant of glacial Lake Assabet and the source of the Sudbury River.

The dramatic evidence of the effect of the glaciers' weight can be seen in Acadia National Park, Maine. Long ago, at the edge of the ocean beneath the glacial ice, the waters carved out a sea cave from the granite. Today the mouth of that cave lies high on the flank of Gorham Mountain, along the Cadillac Cliffs – a silent testament to the immense pressure exerted by glacial ice.

Both the Assabet and Sudbury Rivers arise in Westborough. Each is roughly 31 miles in length, though the Assabet contributes more water to the Concord River. The Assabet takes the more northwesterly route, from the SuAsCo Reservoir. Just a few miles to the east, Cedar Swamp Pond starts the Sudbury River on its way. They combine forces at Egg Rock; the Concord then has another 16 miles to run to the north, into Lowell and the Merrimack River.

The Sudbury and Assabet Rivers converge in Concord, Massachusetts, to create the Concord River. These three Merrimack tributaries together form the SuAsCo watershed. The hikes described in this guidebook are woven together by the threads of the waterways feeding the nearly 80 miles of combined length of these rivers.

Human use of these waterways and the surrounding lands has evolved over time. Between 17,000 and 12,000 years ago, the first humans moved into the area as the glaciers receded. With abundant wildlife but sparse edible vegetation available to them, these nomadic Paleo-Indian hunter-gatherers were mainly meat eaters. Efficient hunters, they may have essentially eliminated the large mammals of the era, while smaller animals and more edible plants invaded from the south. Archaeological evidence shows that the Indians also fished in the waters of the nearby Merrimack.

During the Archaic period, from 10,000 to 3,000 years ago, forests developed toward their current state. In the central uplands of the SuAsCo watershed, the forest included a mix of birch, beech, oak, maple, hemlock and pine. As vegetation spread and diversified, the Archaic people came to depend more and more upon plant life for their food, and they made more permanent settlements.

The Woodlands period began about 3,000 years ago with the arrival of the influence of the Adena, pushed into New England by pressure from peoples of the Southwest and Midwest. As they came to the region, they brought along ceramics and horticulture – corn, beans, squash, pumpkin, and tobacco. In this period, the Algonquin people settled into fertile areas along the streams and rivers of the watershed, practicing farming in addition to hunting and gathering. They regularly burned out the underbrush to facilitate hunting under the remaining hardwoods. The Indian village of Muskataquid, one of the main villages of the Massachusetts tribe, was located on and around Nashawtuc Hill, between the Assabet and Sudbury Rivers, in what is now Concord. These Indians fished and planted crops in spring, then canoed to the Merrimack River and on toward the ocean, finding food and trading with Europeans and other Indians. They dried fish and shellfish to bring back upriver where their crops would be ready for harvest. They also hunted -- for meat and hides.

By the time of first contact with Europeans, permanent settlements and planted fields had appeared. Newly arrived white settlers put the waterways to work for farming and for industry, irrigating crops as well as building dams and mills along rivers and streams. From the 1660s through the 1700s, as colonization spread throughout the area, water-powered mills sprang up in every town. Wherever there was a sufficient flow of water, a mill was likely to be built.

The earliest mills served the most basic of the colonists' needs: saw mills, grist or grain mills, cider and vinegar mills, and oil mills. More complex products came from the mills of the 1800s: shingle mills, box mills, pencil mills, spindle mills, cotton (Hopkinton boasted only the second cotton mill in the country, from 1808), woolen, yarn, carpet and paper mills.

Stone fence
Great Elms / Williams Pond, Harvard (Hike # 17)

Boardwalk from Newtown Road through the wetland
Grassy Pond / Nagog Hill, Acton (Hike # 22)

Water was also vital to certain processes such as tanning and fulling (a process for treating homespun cloth to keep it from unraveling). The old stonework from mill foundations and raceways can be observed in numerous locations on the hikes in this book.

Further evolution in the waterscape came with the creation of reservoirs. For example, the 1898 Fayville Dam in Southborough was built to provide storage for water on its way to Boston from the Wachusett Reservoir in Boylston.

The Indians had established major pathways across Massachusetts, including The Old Connecticut Path and the Old Bay Path, linking Massachusetts Bay and the Connecticut River Valley. Friendly Indians used these paths to bring food to early colonists during the harsh winter. Colonists themselves used these routes for initial exploration and transportation, and built many more miles of roadway as each town developed. Concord's colonial roads included what is now Old Estabrook Road in Estabrook Woods, which survives as a footpath. Carlisle's Minutemen marched down this path to Concord's North Bridge on the eve of the Revolution.

Where road and water met, evolution occurred as well. Indian paths and fords at shallow spots were widened for cart paths. When colonists needed bridges, they sought solid riverbanks, changing the courses of the original paths; later still, improved road-building often straightened the original roads. Foundations remaining from old bridges can be spotted throughout the watershed.

Today our watershed reveals evidence of its past to the hiker in many ways: in the relative youth of the trees (due to the nearly complete clearing of the land during colonial times), in the miles of stone fences that remain from efforts to prepare the land for planting, in overgrown foundations of homes and barns – you'll find them on virtually every hike in this book. Abandoned quarries lie scattered throughout these woods: lime quarries in Concord and Bolton, and granite quarries in Acton and Ashland. In just 400 years the watershed has been transformed from agrarian to industrial to increasingly residential, with the advent of automobiles, good roads and commuting. Despite this, much of the rural beauty remains, as you will discover through these hikes.

> Come, wander with me, for the moonbeams are bright
> On river and forest, o'er mountain and lea.
>
> Charles Jeffreys (1807-1865)

Introduction to the Hikes

Among the hikes presented here, you will find excursions to tiny tributaries, gemlike ponds, vast reservoirs, and the margins of the three rivers themselves. While these suggested hikes range in length from less than two to more than six miles, and in difficulty from easy strolls to more challenging, steeper slopes, you may also adjust your own journey in many ways. Starting from these introductions to the rich variety of conservation properties in our watershed, it's up to you to explore, discover and appreciate.

Sudbury River Watershed

Westborough's Cedar Swamp Pond, the source of the Sudbury River, can be approached on foot but only in winter after many days below freezing. Less than a mile north, however, lies the **Walkup and Robinson Memorial Reservation**, threaded through by a nameless brook whose waters eventually trickle into the Sudbury. The reservation's wide variety of habitats, as well as its human history, are celebrated in a pamphlet available at the trailhead kiosk.

A little further north you'll find **Cedar Hill**, a glacial drumlin topped by a meadow with a wide-ranging view over the hills of Westborough. This property is virtually surrounded by Crane Swamp, and forms one link in the Westborough Charm Bracelet trail network.

Just downstream sprawls **Hopkinton State Park**, providing miles of trails, including the Long Trail around Hopkinton Reservoir, running within earshot of the Sudbury on the northern boundary of the park.

The Sudbury Reservoir and adjacent Callahan State Park cover an extensive area to the east of Crane Swamp. The **Gibbs Mountain / Beebe Pond** section of the State Park offers steep hiking, broad open meadows, and a beauty of a pond surrounded by tranquil forest. You'll enter via the adjacent Sudbury Valley Trustees' Baiting Brook property; the brook leads directly to the Sudbury River, while Beebe Pond drains into Angelica Brook, a tributary of the Foss Reservoir.

The Sudbury River next passes through Wayland, a haven for conservation land. **Hamlen Woods** offers the old Wayland Reservoirs and their resident ducks and beavers; Snake Brook empties these reservoirs into Lake Cochituate and thence to the Sudbury. In the northeast corner of the town, a cluster of properties along several Sudbury River tributaries awaits you -- explore **Upper Mill Brook**'s extensive wetlands, **School House Pond**'s dramatic eskers and **Trout Brook**'s enormous kettleholes. From one corner of the expansive **Weston Town Forest** you can make your way to the placid beauty of Stone's Pond, emptying into vigorously flowing **Hazel Brook**.

Boulders in Indian Brook
Hopkinton State Park, Hopkinton (Hike # 3)

Stone's Pond along Hazel Brook
Hazel Brook / Weston Town Forest, Wayland (Hike # 8)

In the neighboring town of Sudbury you will find lovely **Hop Brook Marsh** and adjacent **Memorial Forest**, with miles of trails through varied habitats. Hop Brook runs north to the Sudbury Valley Trustee's easy-walking **Gray Reservation,** on its way to the Sudbury. On the banks of the river, **Weir Hill** provides a fine view of the waterway from a kettlehole-studded kame plain, while nearby **Round Hill**'s open summit faces south and west, an excellent spot to observe hawk migration.

Finally, in Lincoln you can walk around lovely **Farrar Pond** and scale **Mount Misery**, as well as watch the Sudbury flow by Knacker's Point, just upstream from vast Fairhaven Bay.

Assabet River Watershed

The SuAsCo or Nichols Reservoir is formed by a flood-control dam and covers some 380 acres in Westborough. A network of trails in the **Headwaters Conservation Area** includes a portion of Westborough's Charm Bracelet trail system. Views over the reservoir appear from a distance at the trailhead kiosk; for a closer look, hike down to Osprey Point.

From the far northwest corner of Berlin, explore North Brook as it passes through the boulder-strewn landscape of **Garfield Woods** en route to the town's southern tip, where the brook empties into the Assabet from Wheeler Pond. The ridges and ravines in the interior of this property and the adjacent **Forty Caves** area provide challenging hiking and striking scenery.

Between Berlin and Westborough you'll find Northborough's **Edmund Hill**, through which flows a stream that will feed the Assabet just a half-mile on. The Wachusett Aqueduct also skirts the hill on its way to the Sudbury Reservoir and Sudbury River.

In Hudson, enjoy Danforth Brook's 20-plus-foot drop over **Danforth Falls** – the highest natural waterfall in the Assabet's tributary system. A fine view is also available from the top of Phillips Hill on the same property.

Harvard's **Great Elms** conservation area lies within the upper reaches of the tributary system of Elizabeth Brook, as does adjacent **Williams Pond**. The nearby **Delaney Project**, another flood-control undertaking at the juncture of Harvard, Boxborough and Stow, drains through Delaney Pond to Elizabeth Brook and Assabet Brook before meeting the Assabet River just west of the Stow-Maynard line. An extensive web of trails covers much of the 580-acre state-owned property, running along the reservoir, across numerous streams and atop glacial eskers. **Gardner Hill** sits astride Assabet Brook as well, and provides the opportunity to explore a goodly length of the shoreline of the Assabet River itself.

Visit Heath Hen Meadow Brook from two perspectives: a couple of miles downstream from its Bolton headwaters, at Stow's **Heath Hen Meadow Brook Woodland** Conservation Area, and again at its confluence with Fort Pond Brook in Acton's **Heath Hen Meadow** Conservation Area. Fort Pond Brook then carries its waters on to the Assabet through Warner's Pond in West Concord.

Another source for Warner's Pond waters is the area around unspoiled **Nashoba Pond**, through which both Nonset and Vine Brooks pass into Nashoba Brook. Warner's Pond also collects the waters of Nagog Pond, alongside Acton's **Nagog Hill**, via Nagog and Nashoba Brooks. Adjacent **Grassy Pond** feeds the Fort Pond Brook; a sturdy platform stretches out into the pond to provide a comfortable and serene viewpoint on this lovely spot, while nearby a lengthy boardwalk enables exploration of the neighboring swamp – often right at water level!

Concord River Watershed

The confluence of the Assabet and Sudbury Rivers in Concord at **Egg Rock** is easy to visit, except when water levels are at their highest. Just north of the confluence you will find serene hiking as well as nuggets of human history throughout **Estabrook Woods**, along with a chain of lovely ponds: Bateman's Pond draining to Mink, Mink leading to Hutchins, and all of them conveying their waters via Sawmill Brook to the Concord.

On the south side of the river lies an accessible portion of the 3600-acre **Great Meadows National Wildlife Refuge**, with a trail running parallel to the Concord for about a mile and a half. A bit farther downstream you find dry-season access to the opposite bank via Carlisle's **River Meadows Reservation**, encompassing Greenough Woods and Pond, as well as another segment of the Refuge. East of River Meadows, Mill Brook contributes to the Concord via Bedford's **Minnie Reid** Conservation Area.

Explore Carlisle further at **Great Brook Farm State Park**, with a tour of Meadow Pond and Tophet Swamp. The swamp drains southeast into Page's Brook, one of the feeder streams from Greenough Pond above, while Meadow Pond leads north through Russell's Millpond to River Meadow Brook and the Concord River in Lowell, some 16 miles farther downstream.

Billerica offers the **Vietnam Veteran's Park** and the adjacent **Ralph Hill Woodlot** along the Concord just south of Route 3, with trails through glacier-carved territory rising steeply up to 150 feet above the water's edge, providing one of the last reasonably-unspoiled views before the Concord meets the Merrimack in Lowell.

One of many well-placed benches
Great Meadows National Wildlife Refuge, Concord (Hike # 26)

*You will find something more in woods
than in books.*

*Trees and stones will teach you
that which you can never learn from masters.*

Saint Bernard (1090 - 1153), *Epistle*

20

Sudbury River Watershed

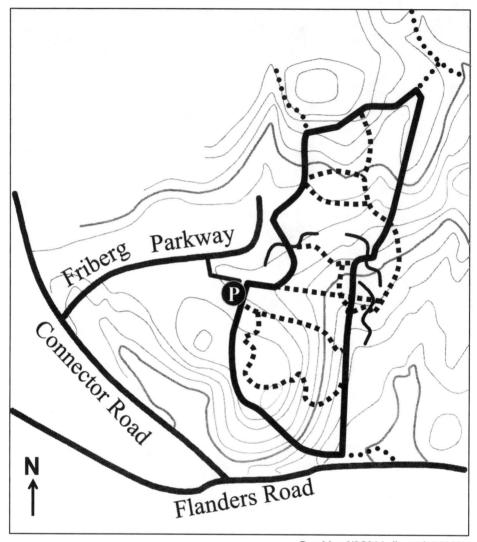

Base Map: USGS Marlborough 1:25,000

Walkup and Robinson, Westborough

▬▬▬	Perimeter loop
▪▪▪▪▪▪	Interior network
•••••••	Other trails
∿∿∿	Stream crossing

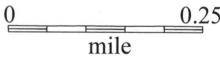

0   0.25

mile

1

Walkup and Robinson Memorial Reservation

Town: Westborough
Rating: Moderate
Distance: 3.1 miles
Hiking Time: 1.5 - 2.5 hours
Maps: USGS Marlborough

Summary: This 62-acre memorial to four generations of a local farming family encompasses hardwood and old pasture uplands, wooded wetland, a pond and open fields. The network of trails provides many possible variations, two of which are described here. The first offering is a moderately easy perimeter loop, with two moderately steep sections; second, consider a meandering interior tour via a series of shorter trail segments covering somewhat more challenging terrain. Total length for the two segments is 3.1 miles.

Trailhead Location: The Walkup Reservation is near the Computer Drive / Research Drive exit off Route 9; it is the first exit west of I-495. Take Connector Road about ½ mile south, then turn left onto Friberg Parkway at the Westborough Business Park sign. The entrance to the reservation is a gravel drive marked by a Sudbury Valley Trustees sign on the right side of the parkway.

When to Visit: This reservation abuts a variety of commercial and industrial buildings, some of which produce significant noise. For those working nearby, the reservation provides a welcome getaway during the week; however, if you plan to visit from further away, consider coming on a weekend or holiday for a quieter experience.

Directions: Perimeter Loop

From the kiosk at the far end of the parking area, descend the stone steps onto the wide Trolley Line trail, the old right-of-way for the Boston-Worcester trolley. After walking a few yards down the trail, turn right onto the red-marked "Front Loop," then take another right at a Y-intersection to continue on the red trail (the blue-marked "Nature Trail" heads off to the left).

Well and Cattle Pass area

Where the trail descends through a long left curve towards the low end of the property, a trail angles off sharply to the right toward a pedestrian entry off Flanders Road, about three minutes away. A stone fence-bounded field lies in front of you at this junction, with cedar trees scattered along the fence line.

Continue to the left on the red trail, beginning a gentle rise alongside the stone fence. At a junction with a trail coming in from the field to the right, continue straight and uphill. Pass by a blue-marked trail to the left ("Upland Knoll"). The red trail levels out as a green trail angles uphill to the left; continue straight on the red trail.

You soon arrive at the site of an old well to the left of the trail; pause and admire the stonework in the terraced walls and steps. The pond to the right of the trail is another lovely spot. You may wish to step across the stream exiting the pond and loop up over the cattle-pass bridge ahead of you (created so that livestock could travel freely from one pasture to another without crossing the trolley line) before returning past the well to the red trail.

The pathway continues straight through the underpass ahead, then rises to a T-junction. Turn right to walk over a footbridge, anchored on both ends by more fine stonework. At the far end of the footbridge, bear left on the red trail, bypassing the blue trail which heads toward another field to the right.

At a trail junction by a post numbered 3, the red trail continues uphill and slightly to the left, while the blue and green trails angle more sharply left. Continue on red. Granite outcrops continue to dot the surroundings.

The steady uphill grows noticeably steeper for a minute, then levels. At a T-junction, the red trail turns to the left. (To the right, a narrow trail leads through the stone fence, off SVT property and downhill over granite ledge to a T-junction with a trail running above a stream. Massive granite formations provide an impressive backdrop. This trail continues in both directions, crossing a footbridge over the stream in each direction to provide connecting links to local office buildings.)

Continue on the red trail, rolling downhill to another T-junction. Here, a green trail leads right; turn left instead to continue on the red trail. The path leads downhill for another few minutes walk before arriving at a four-way trail junction. Turn right on red (green goes straight, blue goes left).

The trail soon bends left and over a wooden footbridge, passing over the stream and through forested wetland where red maples flourish. Just over the bridge, continue straight on red (green goes left along the stream). After descending a series of stone steps laid into the granite outcrop, bear right on the Trolley Line trail to return to the kiosk and parking area.

Directions: Interior Network

From the kiosk at the far end of the parking area, descend the stone steps onto the wide Trolley Line trail. A few yards down the trail, turn right onto the red-marked "Front Loop." At the next Y-intersection, turn left onto the blue-marked "Nature Trail." A green-marked trail shortly heads off to the left; you continue straight on the blue trail to begin a steep ascent through a dense hemlock grove.

The trail levels out and curves around the oak- and pine-crowned summit before descending the far side. At a T-junction, turn left onto the red trail, then left again a few dozen steps away to head back uphill on green, climbing steadily between a wooded slope uphill to the left and the Trolley Line downhill to the right. The trail levels out just before rejoining the blue-marked nature trail.

Note: Just before rejoining the blue trail, you may notice a laminated page hanging from a young pine to your left. This is one of several copies of a tribute to Lawrence Walkup by his friend Geoff Christian that are scattered about the property.

Bear right on the blue trail, then right again on red to arrive back at the Trolley Line, just east of the kiosk and parking area. Turn right on the Trolley Line trail, then take the first trail to the left, up a series of granite steps to the red trail. At the next junction, where the red trail goes left ("Jogging Trail"), turn right onto the green trail. The stream runs alongside the trail to the left for a brief distance.

At a Y-junction, with the stone cattle-pass bridge visible ahead through the trees, bear left, then left again onto the red trail. Continue on red across a wooden footbridge, then bear right on the far side of the bridge, onto the green trail (red goes left).

The green trail curves around to the left and slightly uphill to the edge of a meadow. Continue to curve left along the meadow's border, past a granite memorial bench, and then a wooden bench (the latter is the more comfortable spot for a break). Ahead is a tall pine marking a multi-trail intersection. Follow the green and blue trail markers across the intersection and back into the woods.

At the next junction, continue straight on blue (green goes left). The path leads uphill past a lone chunk of granite to another junction. Continue straight on green ("Gorge Trail") as blue goes left.

The trail climbs steadily uphill, becoming steeper as the gorge narrows briefly. The uphill grade then eases as the landscape opens up at the top of the gorge. At the next two junctions, turn left on red. At a four-way trail intersection, go straight, now on green.

The green trail continues downhill through mixed pine and deciduous with an under-story of pine. At a T-junction, turn left on blue. Just ahead, turn left again on blue at the next junction (green goes straight uphill into the gorge that you just visited).

The path leads uphill on a moderate slope, becoming a bit steeper just before arriving at the lip of a steep down-slope in front of you. The trail bends left here, but you may wish to pause and enjoy the view across to the far slope (and perhaps catch your breath).

Continue left and briefly uphill. The trail then descends on a moderate slope back to the four-way intersection. Go straight across onto the red trail to return to the Trolley Line where you began the series of interior loops.

2

Cedar Hill

Town: Northborough
Rating: Moderate
Distance: 2.4 miles, with optional extensions
Hiking Time: 1.5 - 2 hours
Maps: USGS Marlborough

Summary: The varied habitat and serenity offered by this hike provide an enjoyable contrast to the light industrial and commercial area in which the trailhead is located. At the top of the drumlin lies a grassy field with a fine view to the south and west. The moderately easy hike described here is 2.4 miles long, with additional extensions available as part of Westborough's Charm Bracelet trail system. You may also take a shorter, more direct route to the top of Cedar Hill.

Trailhead Location: From the junction of Routes 20 and 495 in Marlborough, drive 1.4 miles west on 20, and turn left onto Hayes Memorial Drive. Turn right at the next stop sign, onto Bartlett Street, then take the next, sharp left onto Cedar Hill Street. Turn right after 0.3 miles, into the parking lot of a commercial building at #360. Park in one of several spaces reserved for the Sudbury Valley Trustees (SVT); the reserved spaces are those closest to Cedar Hill Street, and are marked with individual SVT signposts.

Directions

As you face the building at 360 Cedar Hill Street, the trail begins directly to your left. Look for a signpost at the far edge of the mowed strip of grass bordering the parking lot. The SVT trail marker (white diamond) points you along the edge of the mowed area to the right of the signpost. Follow additional such signposts along the mowed border.

At the 4th marker, the mowed area narrows to a slender trail atop a winding embankment. The trail passes a small, cattail-fringed pond on the right before arriving at the SVT kiosk and trail map. The trail then bends to the left around the far side of the kiosk to pass under a power line, across a train track and through a stand of mixed pine, cedar and deciduous trees to a tranquil field. At the far side of the field, follow the trail as it curves towards the woods.

Base Map: USGS Marlborough 1:25,000

Cedar Hill, Northborough

———— Main route

••••••• Other trails

〰〰 Stream crossing

▬ ▬ Westborough Charm Bracelet Trail

N
↑

0   0.5

mile

The trail winds through an area of younger cedar and deciduous trees, across a rocky-bedded streamlet and into taller, older pines. Occasional white-diamond SVT and red-triangle Northborough trail markers lead you gradually uphill as the trail grows rockier and steeper, passing a big flat-topped boulder that can seem magnetic in its ability to attract younger hikers to climb atop it.

Just past this boulder is a Y-junction (A on map). A signpost gives you a choice between a direct climb to Cedar Hill (0.2 miles) or a more roundabout route in the direction of Walker Street. The hike described here takes you to the left, on the longer 'scenic' route. Additional white diamond trail markers indicate that you are now on Westborough's Charm Bracelet Trail.

Downhill to the left in irregular ranks march closely spaced trunks of tall, slender pine, through which a view of hills against the horizon to the northeast is visible. As you cross over a stone fence and in among the pines, note the clear demarcation between this area and the mixed growth you have now left behind. The stone fence also marks the boundary of the SVT property.

Continue downhill into a low-lying mix of deciduous including birch. Cross a railed metal-mesh span over a streamlet to a dirt road and a Charm Bracelet trail marker. The trail to the left (toward Walker Street) is closed as of this writing. Proceed to the right along the dirt road, in the direction of Lyman Street. Crane Swamp, spreading off to your left, is protected within the Westborough Wildlife Management Area.

The next trail marker appears on your right after a few minutes of walking along the dirt road. Turn right, away from the dirt road and into the trees. The trail proceeds gradually uphill in an area dominated by oak. At the next trail junction, turn right through a stone fence gap and back on to SVT property.

Note: Continuing left at this junction enables you to follow the Charm Bracelet Trail through another part of the Wildlife Management Area. The route runs downhill across the tip of Little Crane Swamp, then fairly steeply up and over another glacial ridge to fields and roads beyond.

As you pass through the stone fence, note another dramatic change in vegetation. You leave behind oak in favor of pine, cedar and mixed deciduous; low-growing juniper also decorates the sides of the grassy path. The wide trail is open to the sky but intimately enclosed on either side by thick growth. The path climbs gently but continuously upward.

View from the summit

A birdhouse ahead of you on the trail marks your arrival at the field that tops Cedar Hill. Head for the small boulder in the center of the field for a good spot from which to enjoy the view spreading out to the south and west. You may notice a variety of overgrown apple trees in the vicinity of the field, and perhaps smell the scent of their blossoms or fallen fruit depending on the season.

When you are ready to return to the parking area, continue along the trail past the boulder and away from the field. The way down becomes a bit steeper, moving down a brief series of gently curved switchbacks, then over a straighter, rockier stretch leading back to a familiar trail junction (A). Follow the sign to 'field' to return to the trailhead and parking lot by your original route.

A perfect mid-summer's day -- cool, sunny, a few billows of cottony cumulus decorating the cerulean sky, and my nose delighting to the scent of ... lilacs? How incongruous -- they faded months ago, didn't they? Myriad bees and butterflies were well aware of the blooms in question, and now I have garnered my tasty little tidbit of knowledge for the day: The perfume arises from milkweed blossoms, which I had never before encountered.

- Notes from author's journal

Spring blossoms

3

Hopkinton State Park

Town: Hopkinton
Rating: Challenging
Distance: 6.5 miles
Hiking Time: 3 - 4 hours
Maps: USGS Marlborough / Milford

Summary: A 6.5-mile circumnavigation of Hopkinton Reservoir, including views of islands, ponds and streams amid a boulder-strewn landscape just south of the Sudbury River. The Pipeline Trail segment will stretch your legs as you climb over Saddle Hill, but the serene series of ponds at the tail end of the route are worth the extra effort.

Trailhead Location: From the junction of Routes 135 and 85 in Hopkinton, drive north on Route 85. After 1¼ miles, turn right (east) onto Rafferty Road, and immediately left into a boat ramp parking area.

Directions

From the parking lot, head north toward the water, then continue around the reservoir to your right on the Reservoir Run trail. After about a mile (20-30 minutes walking), turn right at a T-junction to Howe Street, then turn left along the road. At the driveway of a water treatment building, head back into woods along the reservoir, continuing around to the dam. You may have to climb back up to the road briefly to negotiate a culvert.

Turn left onto the path across the dam. At the far end, turn right and follow the Oval Trail downhill parallel to the beautifully constructed stone spillway draining the reservoir. This trail leads you toward one of the park's roadways. At a T-junction, turn right to cross the road. Walk along the road to your right briefly, then turn left off the road before the waterway, onto the Long Trail.

A short distance ahead, the Long Trail heads left, into the woods. The trail takes you through an area strewn with boulders. Just after crossing a stream, the trail intersects a wide dirt track (Aikens Road). Continue straight and uphill past more boulders, including a particularly immense specimen that can loom eerily through winter-bare trees.

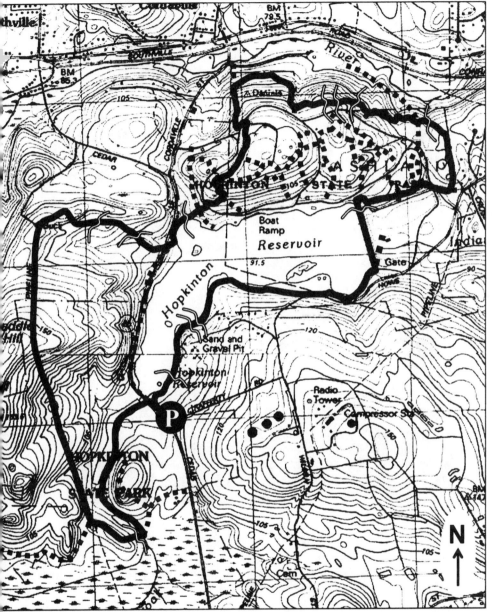

Base Maps: USGS Marlborough/Milford 1:25,000

Hopkinton State Park, Hopkinton

──────── Main route
▪▪▪▪▪▪▪ Other trails
〜〜 Stream crossing

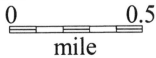

0   0.5
mile

N
↑

Island from Vista Trail

The trail crosses a series of streams. Where a trail heads left to the nearby roadway, continue ahead and then down a moderately steep slope. The trail then curves around the base of the hill to a T-junction with a wider path; turn left onto the Aikens Trail. You'll soon climb back up to the park roadway. Turn left along the road, passing by a gate, then take the next drive to the right; turn right almost immediately onto the Wachusett Trail. Follow this path south, continuing ahead where the Caesar Trail heads left near a parking area – you are now on the Rock Road Trail. Follow this path through its junction with the Loop Trail, bearing left and downhill to stay on Rock Road.

Take the next trail to your right, then walk through a parking lot to Ash Street. Bear left across the pavement to pick up the Vista Trail, which leads you to another lovely view across the reservoir. If the water is not too high, follow this trail around to the right and across a stream until you emerge onto Route 85. (If the trail is flooded, retrace your steps to the nearest trail junction, turn left on the Foxtrot Trail and follow it out to the entrance road. Turn left to 85, then left again to walk along the road.)

At this point you may choose to follow 85 back to Rafferty Road and the parking area. However, you might consider extending your hike by bearing left across 85 from the Vista Trail onto a path heading steadily uphill. About a half-mile from the road, at the top of the climb, turn left at a T-junction onto the wide Pipeline Trail. (This area is experiencing development encroachment, but continues to be passable as of this writing.)

The sometimes-wet trail takes you past the summit of Saddle Hill, then down its flank to a junction with the Duck Pond Trail. Turn left. A bridge carries you over a stream; turn left again at the T-junction on the far side. The trail now runs alongside a series of ponds, their beauty punctuated by a variety of boulders.

The trail ultimately leads you back to Route 85. Cross the road and turn right; the parking lot from which you began is just a short distance away.

Trailside erratics

4

Gibbs Mountain / Beebe Pond

Town: Framingham
Rating: Challenging (steepness)
Distance: 3.7 miles
Hiking Time: 1.5 - 2.5 hours
Maps: USGS Framingham

Summary: This 3.7-mile hike offers a delightful combination of mountain, meadow and pond. While the route includes a moderately challenging uphill climb along the flank of Gibbs Mountain, the balance of the hike easily circumnavigates a peaceful meadow and pristine tree-girdled Beebe Pond. Many additional miles of trail may be accessed throughout Callahan State Park, on both sides of Edmands Road.

Trailhead Location: From Route 30 in Framingham, take Pine Hill Road north to Parmenter Road in Southborough and turn east. Across the Framingham border, the road becomes Edmands. Continue for one mile to the corner of Edmands and Nixon Roads, where parking for several cars is available in a gravel area on the west side of the intersection. (Additional parking, for the State Park, is available about one third of a mile further west on Edmands.)

This hike starts from the trailhead kiosk for the Sudbury Valley Trustee's Welch Reservation, located just off the south side of Edmands Road, two minutes' walk west on Edmands from the corner of Nixon and Edmands.

Directions

From the kiosk, walk southeast on a tree and brush-lined lane between fields. After crossing a footbridge over a Baiting Brook tributary, bear right at a Y-intersection, then continue straight and uphill. When your trail reaches the wide pipeline right-of-way, turn right over the stream then left back into the woods; take an immediate right onto the Wren Trail and continue uphill. Go straight at the next junction (the Rocky Road trail); the trail soon heads downhill. Bear right at a Y-junction onto the Red-Tail Trail and immediately cross a stream. Follow this trail straight through a 4-way junction, continuing on to Edmands Road, well west of the parking area.

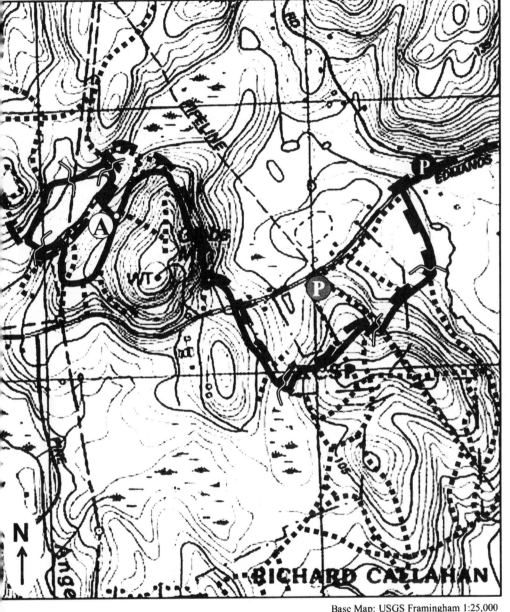

Base Map: USGS Framingham 1:25,000

Gibbs Mountain / Beebe Pond, Framingham

Main route	
Other trails	
Stream crossing	
Bay Circuit Trail	

N

0   0.5

mile

At Edmands Road, continue straight across. After passing by a field, begin a moderately steep climb along the flank of Gibbs Mountain. Your trail is marked by bright blue triangles with a black backpacker symbol, indicating the Backpacker Trail. The Bay Circuit Trail also follows this route.

Pass by a trail angling sharply uphill toward the summit, then bear left at a Y-junction. Where Backpacker and Bay Circuit Trail markers point sharply right and downhill, continue straight. At the edge of a field, turn left (A on map) to walk around its perimeter, rising to a lovely view of the local area.

As the trail turns downhill, bear right at a Y-junction, then continue straight at the next two trail junctions. The last of these is near a granite stele marking the Framingham – Marlborough border.

At a 4-way junction, turn left to pass through a stone fence gap into the woods on the Pine Tree Loop trail. This trail continues straight, but first detour briefly down-slope to your right, to the water's edge for a lovely view of Beebe Pond – a serene spot for a rest break. Lily pads abound in summer; when a breeze lifts their edges, a flash of red shows underneath their green skirts.

Continue on the Pine Tree Loop, stepping across the spillway exiting the pond. A multiple trail junction is just ahead, near an old chimney. To continue around Beebe Pond, turn right. Watch for a point at which the trail passes through a stone fence gap, and turn right at an easy-to-miss trail junction just ahead, continuing on the Pine Tree Loop.

After crossing a footbridge over the pond's feeder stream, turn right on a wide pipeline track. At the edge of the field ahead, turn left and uphill; at the next T-junction, turn left again at A, into the woods.

Continue straight at the next two trail junctions, then bear right and uphill as you rejoin the Backpacker and Bay Circuit Trails. Retrace your original route back along the Backpacker Trail and across Edmands Road.

Go straight at the first major trail junction past Edmands, then turn left onto the Wren Trail. Follow the Bay Circuit Trail markers back to the trailhead kiosk, then turn right (east) along Edmands to return to the parking area.

Beebe Pond

5

Hamlen Woods

Town: Wayland
Rating: Moderate
Distance: 3.0 miles
Hiking Time: 1 - 2 hours
Maps: USGS Framingham

Summary: A comfortable 3-mile ramble through tranquil forest from Hamlen Woods to the Pond Loop trail at the top of Reeves Hill, including an intriguing transit of an old reservoir showing evidence of beaver activity. The main trail is easy with some steeper sections on the way up Reeves Hill. Additional trails are available across Rice Road on Town of Wayland conservation land; a climb to the hidden summit of Turkey Hill is a good leg-stretcher.

Trailhead Location: From I-95/ Route 128, follow Route 20 West. Just past the Weston/Wayland town line, bear left onto Old Connecticut Path. After 0.6 mile, turn left onto Rice Road. Continue for 1.5 miles to the Wayland Conservation Commission parking area on the right (west) side of Rice Road.

Directions

Follow the trail from the kiosk at the parking area, bearing right at a T-junction to cross over a spillway between two portions of the Old Wayland Reservoirs. Across the spillway, turn left at junction 1 (on map) onto the trail along the water's edge past a bench with a lovely view; the path soon becomes a narrow causeway.

The causeway leads across one end of a small granite island crowned by pines. Beavers felling trees have left behind their characteristic pencil-point trunk stubs along the island's shores. Cross a wooden footbridge over a channel between the two ponds to regain the mainland.

The trail, now wide and level, continues along the water's edge. Occasional boardwalks and a footbridge help you cross a few of the wetter areas. The trail narrows as it squeezes past a cliff, home to an "outstanding community of ferns, mosses and lichen. Please do not climb on the cliff." (from a leaflet posted at trailside).

Hamlen Woods, Wayland

Base Map: USGS Framingham 1:25,000

▬▬▬ Main route
▬ ▬ Other trails
〜 Stream crossing
B o Posted junction marker

0   0.5

mile

Just past the cliff is an unmarked 4-way trail junction (2 on map). Head across the junction and up a series of log steps. You have now moved from Town of Wayland to SVT property.

The path continues uphill, curving past a massive and beautifully moss-covered granite ledge. Continue straight at intersection B. The trail follows alongside a stone fence to your right.

The next trail junction, marked by a pair of red pentagons, is Intersection C. Turn sharply to the right and downhill, below a high granite outcrop to the left on a narrow track, soon passing through a stone fence gap.

Follow the red-marked trail right at junction V, left at W, then right at the next, unmarked intersection a short distance ahead. The trail now zigzags along parallel to a lovely series of stone fences, rolling sometimes steeply over the hilly terrain. As the path levels to run past a dead-end street, bear right through a stone fence gap to continue on the trail heading away from the road.

Bear left as a trail comes in from your right (junction X), moving into an area of birch (amid other trees) near the high point of the local terrain. Watch for a double-trunked tree at junction Y and bear right, toward the Pond Loop trail. Bear right at a T-junction; small wooden signs as well as red-painted blazes now mark your trail.

The trail soon turns left to run past a pond, then right at a T-junction at the far end of the pond. Though trail signs soon point you right again on a narrow trail, continue straight on the wider trail for another couple of minutes to a wide Y-junction, then bear right. The trail circles a wetland, crossing a pair of streams that drain the wetland down a steep slope to the southeast. You will soon find yourself back at junction X; turn right and retrace your steps to intersection 2 by the Old Wayland Reservoirs.

Rather than turning right around the reservoirs, continue straight, crossing a footbridge over a stream. This wide trail will return you to the parking lot, along the eastern shore of the old reservoir.

Old Wayland Reservoir

*Near the top of Reeves Hill, tracing along the stone fences,
I heard a barred owl for the first time in my 46 years. I had
almost decided not to climb the hill that late afternoon, but here
was ample reward. I sat, listened and returned downhill with a
new tune in my head: "Who cooks for you? Who cooks for you-all?"*
- Notes from author's journal

Reeves Hill stone fence line

6

Upper Mill Brook

Town: Wayland
Rating: Easy
Distance: 3.2 miles
Hiking Time: 1 - 2 hours
Maps: USGS Framingham / Maynard

Summary: The Upper Mill Brook area includes ponds, wetlands and streams threading among glacial ridges. This large, contiguous conservation area teems with birds and other wildlife. While most of the 3.2-mile hike is moderately easy, there is one steep section -- the path out to Claypit Hill Road runs over a narrow, slanted trail crossing the base of a moderately steep ridge, with wetland to one side. Waterproof boots and a walking stick may prove useful.

Trailhead Location: Follow Route 126 (Concord Road) north from the light at the junction of 126 and 20 in the center of Wayland. One mile north on your right is Peace Lutheran Church at 107 Concord Road. The church allows its parking lot to be used for public parking when it is not being used for church activities; therefore, please avoid parking on Sunday morning. There are also footpath entrances from Concord Road, Glezen Lane and Claypit Hill Road.

Directions

The Sudbury Valley Trustees trailhead is located at the back of the church property, beyond the far corner of a small fenced-in play yard. The hike begins to the right of the Upper Mill Brook sign, on a narrow trail hemmed in on both sides with dense undergrowth. At a four-way trail junction (1 on map), continue straight to a field, with a pond in front of you.

Turn left alongside the pond, leaving the water on your right. At the far end of the pond, just before a wide footbridge, turn left, moving away from the pond to cross over a long, narrow footbridge. Bear left at a Y-junction under tall pines. You will shortly arrive at a 4-way junction (marked "R") near a second pond. The trail to your left leads out to Concord Road (Route 126); you take the first right leading away from this pond.

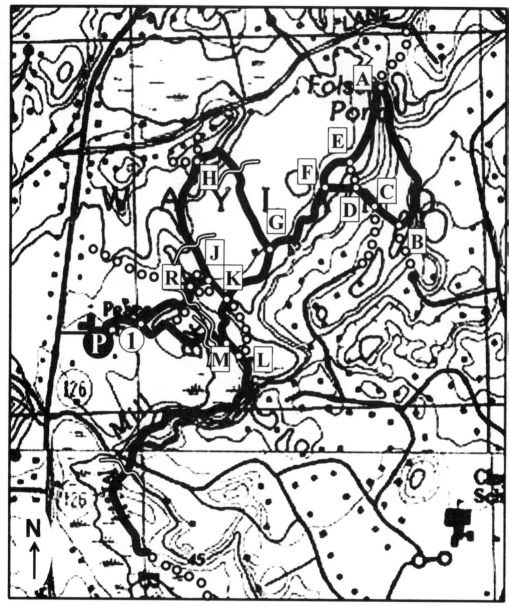

Upper Mill Brook, Wayland

Base Map: USGS Framingham/Maynard 1:25,000

— Main route

○○○○○ Other trails

∿ Stream crossing

[A]○ Posted junction marker

N ↑

0 .... 0.5
mile

At the next trail junction (J), turn left and continue ahead to a wooden footbridge. To your right is a beaver dam, where a beaver pipe has been installed to maintain the water at a level that prevents damage to nearby properties. Just past the bridge, continue straight at a junction, walking along a narrow ridge between wetland areas. The ridge fades as the ground rises and dries out on both sides.

At a Y-junction, follow yellow trail markers to the right. The trail rolls up and down amid generations of pine and oak, with an extensive swamp to the right. Continue straight at the next trail junction as a trail angles off to the left, then bear right a few steps farther on at intersection H.

The trail soon crosses a boardwalk and bridge, running through wetlands and over a brook. The trail continues to curve to the right around the swamp, through dense underbrush, grasses and reeds.

At Intersection G take the left fork, following orange trail markers. After a slight uphill, the trail curves left and levels alongside a short section of tumbledown stone fence to the left of the trail.

Follow the main trail as it curves around the base of a hill. At an unmarked Y intersection near a small pond, bear left; make note of this unmarked intersection for your return trip. You are now on Town of Wayland land.

Intersection F is a few steps ahead. Turn left at F, still following orange trail markers, with the pond still to your left. The trail soon swings away from the pond and uphill to intersection E. Turn left onto the yellow-marked loop trail.

The path takes you through pine and oak with a hill rising to the right of the trail. Soon the trail begins to rise, and you arrive at Intersection A. Bear right to continue on the yellow trail. The trail leads along a series of ridgelines. You will bear right at Intersections B and C.

At Intersection D, turn left onto an orange-marked trail to begin your return to Sudbury Valley Trustees land and the main hike. Turn left at the next Y-intersection (unmarked); wetland is visible at a distance off to your right. A short distance ahead, a trail comes in from the right to merge with your trail. This marks your return to the path that leads back to Intersection G.

At Intersection G, continue straight up a short, steep rise, quickly descending again through a stone fence into denser pine woods. The trail rises again to Intersection K, atop a ridge running to your right and left. Continue straight, descending the other side of the ridge on the yellow pentagon trail. The level path soon leads to Intersection M. Bear left to continue on yellow.

Crossing by the beaver dam at Upper Mill Brook, I spot a rock on the move ... or rather, a painted turtle. The turtle pauses briefly, gazes straight at me as I perform my camera antics, then proceeds along the trail as before. Quite the photogenic reptile, it evinces not the slightest interest in (nor any concern about) this large, shell-less creature in its path -- and why should it? ·

- Notes from author's journal

Painted turtle

At Intersection L, go straight on the red triangle trail (yellow goes left, looping back to K).

On this level path, bear right at an unmarked Y-junction, then right again a few steps farther along. The trail from this point becomes quite narrow, sloping along the base of the ridge running steeply up to your left. Varied and uneven footing takes you along the edge of the extensive Mill Brook wetland to the right of the trail. Trees become useful handholds at a few spots along this section of the trail, and occasional boardwalks assist under foot.

A final set of boardwalks leads you into a closely overgrown section of trail with water on both sides, then back into pine and oak woods. Private property notices appear to the right of the trail as it rises moderately steeply above the waterway to the right. The trail cuts across the slope to emerge on Claypit Hill Road at the trailhead, about 0.2 miles east of Concord Road (Route 126).

Cross Claypit Hill Road onto the continuation of the red triangle trail directly across the street from the SVT trailhead. The trail winds through wetlands and woods, over boardwalks and small bridges, to a lovely sweeping curve of boardwalk extending out over the swamp about 5 minutes in from Claypit Hill Road. This represents the *turn-around point* for the hike suggested here.

> If you wish to extend the hike, the trail continues on to a T-junction about 5 minutes away. Turning right and walking for a few more minutes would take you to Glen Road across from #33, about 0.2 miles in from Concord Road (Route 126). To the left, the trail ends on Plains Road 0.4 miles west of Claypit Hill Road.

Continuing from the *turn-around point* at the long boardwalk, retrace your route across Claypit Road to intersection M. Turn left at M. After crossing a pair of footbridges, you will find yourself back at the far side of the first pond encountered on this hike. Bear left, then right around the pond to return to the Peace Lutheran parking lot.

7

School House Pond / Trout Brook

Town: Wayland
Rating: Moderate
Distance: 2.0 miles
Hiking Time: 45 min. - 1 hour
Maps: USGS Maynard

Summary: On this two-part hike you encounter the effects of two indomitable forces of nature: glaciers and beavers. Highlights include lovely views across Schoolhouse Pond – created by a beaver dam – and glacial kettle holes in the kame plain above Trout Brook, in addition to the pleasures of ridge-walking high atop glacial eskers. Much of the 2-mile route follows the course of the Bay Circuit Trail, between the southern end of Schoolhouse Pond and Trout Brook to the north. You will encounter quite a bit of moderately steep climbing and descending.

Trailhead Location: Follow Route 126 north from the light at the junction of 126 and 20 in the center of Wayland. After 2.5 miles, turn left onto Sherman's Bridge Road, and left again onto Alpine Road. Park at the 90° curve in Alpine Road, by the ball field.

Directions

To begin the Schoolhouse Pond segment, walk along the left side of the ball field next to the woods. Enter the woods by the Castle Hill Conservation Area sign (by third base). The level trail passes through dense underbrush, then curves into an area of mature pine. Bear right as a trail comes in from private property to the left.

Go straight at a Y-junction. The trail crosses a wooden footbridge by a small beaver dam, with a larger dam behind it. Continue straight (south) and uphill with the slope of an esker rising steeply to your left. The Great Meadows National Wildlife Refuge stretches off to your right.

As the trail descends to a gas pipeline crossing, turn left and follow the pipeline across a wetland to a saddle point at the south end of Schoolhouse Pond. (In wet seasons, this segment may be impassable.)

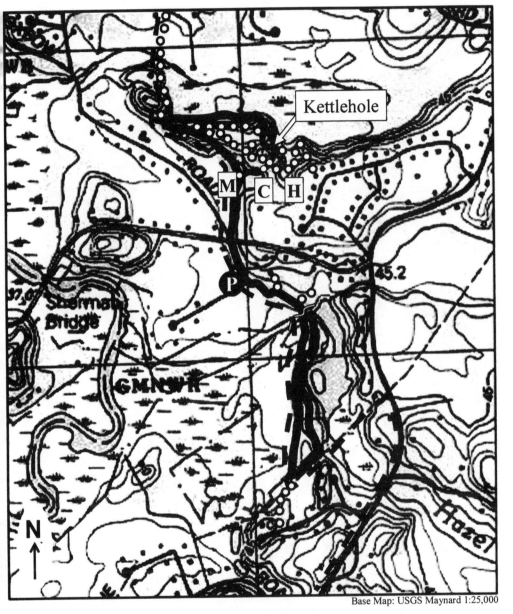

Kettlehole

M C H

P

45.2

45

Sherman Bridge

GMNWR

Hazel

N

Base Map: USGS Maynard 1:25,000

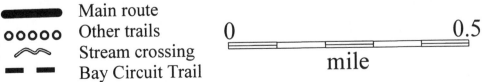

School House Pond / Trout Brook, Wayland

Main route
Other trails
Stream crossing
Bay Circuit Trail

0   0.5
mile

School House Pond

The trail continues left and steeply uphill to run along the top of the esker, parallel to the lower trail that you followed earlier. Enjoy viewing the dramatic drops on both sides, with School House Pond stretching expansively to your right.

Trace the ridgeline until it descends to re-join your original path. A short distance north, bear right and uphill onto another ridgeline. Beaver-cut stumps provide evidence of the animals' ongoing activity. The trail soon descends toward the large beaver dam above the footbridge you crossed earlier. Return to the parking area the way you came.

To continue on to Trout Brook, follow Alpine Road out to the corner of Oxbow and Sherman's Bridge. There is a right-of-way access to the conservation area from Sherman's Bridge Road just beyond its intersection with Oxbow Road.

Look for a trail map box on a post with a yellow triangle pointing the way into the forest past a large sign for the Trout Brook Conservation Area (TBCA). The trail eases gently downhill through tall pines, soon leveling off amid young deciduous undergrowth. After a wooden TBCA sign, the trail drops briefly but steeply to a junction marked M. Bear left, following the trail as it leads you uphill to the top of the kame plain.

The trail descends toward the Trout Brook wetlands to a junction. The Bay Circuit Trail continues straight (usually flooded past a footbridge about a tenth of a mile ahead); you turn right onto a trail that runs just above the wetlands. The path curves around the base of the upland to your right, eventually climbing steeply back uphill. An enormous kettlehole lies just ahead, created by a huge chunk of ice left behind when the glaciers retreated from this area. Follow the trail that skirts it along the eastern (left) side. The path quickly becomes a ridge-top trail between this and another kettle hole.

Bear left at the junction marked H, then immediately right at junction C. The trail brings you back to junction M; bear left to return to the trailhead, then continue across the road to Alpine Road and the parking area.

I cannot say for certain why I love ridgeline trails so much. Perhaps it's that top-of-the-world feeling, along with a touch of adrenaline thanks to the steep gradients at hand to left and to right. In any case, it was a special treat to discover one day a decrepit yet serviceable chair thoughtfully placed under a tree, with School House Pond spread out for contemplation far below. The calming influence of such a view from a comfortable seat provided a welcome counterpoint to the exertion required to reach it.
                                            - Notes from author's journal

8

Hazel Brook / Weston Town Forest

Town: Wayland
Rating: Moderate
Distance: 4.0 miles
Hiking Time: 1.5 - 2.5 hours
Maps: USGS Maynard

Summary: This 4-mile hike traverses a small portion of Weston's 65-mile trail network, crossing into Wayland for a look at lovely Stone's Pond along Hazel Brook. A variety of streams, wetlands and ponds punctuate the quiet woodland paths.

Trailhead Location: From the lights at the junction of Routes 20, 27 and 126 in Wayland center, drive north 1.3 miles on 126, then turn right on Glezen Lane. After ¾ mile, turn right on Draper, then another 0.7 mile further along, turn left on Old Weston Road. Park in the cul-de-sac at the end of the road.

Directions

Enter the woods between a fire hydrant and an overgrown metal gate. Follow the path out to a trail junction (A on map) in a small meadow; then turn left. After crossing a stream, you will find yourself walking alongside a lovely wide field guarded by a pair of enormous pine trees. Watch for a trail leading to the left partway along the field, before the barn, and follow it north, away from the field.

Continue straight at a Y-junction, then make your way across a deeply cut stream. Bear left and downhill at the next junction, and continue on to Sudbury Road. Cross the road, then turn right to walk along the road past one house; turn left at the crest of a small rise to walk along a right-of-way (marked by the green pine tree of a Weston trail sign) heading north between two private properties.

After returning into the woods, continue straight at the first trail junction (B), and straight again at next intersection (marked with a 7 high up on a tree). Bear left at an unnumbered intersection (C), and left again at intersection 6, where two trails head off to the right.

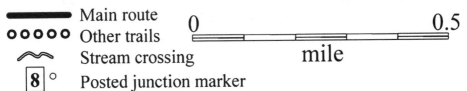

Base Map: USGS Maynard 1:25,000

Hazel Brook / Weston Town Forest, Wayland/Weston

▬▬▬	Main route	
○○○○○	Other trails	
⌒⌒	Stream crossing	
8°	Posted junction marker	

0   0.5

mile

Pines in the pasture

The charming landscape which I saw this morning, is indubitably made up of some twenty or thirty farms. Miller owns this field, Locke that, and Manning the woodland beyond. But none of them own the landscape. There is a property in the horizon which no man has but he whose eye can integrate all the parts, that is the poet. This is the best part of these men's farms, yet to this land deeds give them no title.

Ralph Waldo Emerson, *Essays, Nature*

At intersection 5, bear right at a Y-junction then continue straight past a narrow trail to your right; follow the wider trail as it bears right. Turn left at intersection 4, right at the T-junction marked with a 1, then left at 2. Continue ahead as two trails in succession head right. You enter Sudbury Valley Trustees (SVT) property by a stone fence near an open field. Go straight through the stone fence to a T-junction a few yards away on your left, where you will spot a white diamond-shaped SVT trail marker, pointing you into the woods.

Cross a streamlet on a stepping-stone path, then continue uphill, bearing right at a junction near the top of the slope. Continue straight at the next junction with a trail angling sharply left (D); just ahead, bear left as another trail drops downhill to the right. The trail levels at a Y-junction, then crosses a stream. The path emerges from the woods to cross a grassy meadow below a house. At the far side, bear right into the trees and cross a stream running over the path. Continue on the wide main trail as side trails intersect it, crossing another stream on the way. You soon arrive alongside lovely Stone's Pond, a fine place for a rest.

When you are done enjoying this serene spot, retrace your route across meadow and stream. Bear right at a Y-junction past the second stream and head uphill, bypassing two trails to the left; disregard an SVT trail marker pointing left at D. At the top of the hill, continue straight to pass through a stone fence ahead, leaving SVT property and re-entering Weston Town Forest. Just to your right before you cross the fence, a granite stele marks the boundary between Wayland and Weston.

At the next T-junction, turn right onto a wide track, which continues a large loop you covered part of earlier. Where the trail branches straight and left (a tennis court may be visible – or audible – through the trees to your right), turn left and downhill. Take the next trail to the right, then bear left at a Y-junction onto a narrow path.

This trail segment crosses a stream and passes below a large granite outcrop. When you find yourself back at B, continue straight, and straight again at 7, then turn right at the next, unnumbered junction (C). Climb a small hill, continuing straight at a trail junction to curve past a pile of granite boulders and over a stone fence. The trail then parallels the stone fence, passing by a meadow and along a narrow right of way to return to Sudbury Road.

Angle to the right across the road and into the woods. Follow the trail around a small pond, crossing a ridge and a stream as you go. Continue straight and uphill at a trail junction past the stream. Where the path descends sharply, you are nearing a familiar meadow from the early stage of your hike. Turn right at a T-junction to walk alongside the field. Re-cross the stream at the far end of the field, and turn right at junction A to return to the Old Weston Road cul-de-sac.

9

Hop Brook / Memorial Forest

Town: Sudbury
Rating: Easy
Distance: 3.4 miles
Hiking Time: 1.5 - 2 hours
Maps: USGS Maynard / Framingham

Summary: A ramble over easy terrain, beginning with the lovely Hop Brook Marsh conservation area and extending along Cranberry and Hop Brooks into Memorial Forest. Glacial features abound, including winding eskers and vernal pools formed from kettle holes. The suggested route totals 3.4 miles; you also have a variety of options to extend your hike throughout Memorial Forest.

Trailhead Location: From the junction of Hudson and Dutton Roads in Sudbury, drive 1.3 miles south on Dutton. The Hop Brook parking area is on the right (west) side of the street, and has room for 2-3 cars; additional cars may park along the roadside. In addition, the Sudbury Valley Trustees maintain a trailhead with off-road parking for 8-10 cars, located a half-mile further south on Dutton.

Directions

From the Hop Brook parking area, head past the gate into the woods on a wide track. Follow the main track past various side trails (including junctions 1 and 2 on map) until it curves to the right along the Hop Brook wetlands. Turn left at the next trail junction to a bridge over the brook – a lovely place to pause and enjoy the extensive view in both directions.

Continue across the Hop Brook bridge and the boardwalk beyond. As the trail rises to a Y-junction (3), bear left and uphill over a rock-studded section of trail. A boggy section follows, with a pair of boardwalks provided to aid your passage. The trail soon rises to another junction (4); bear left.

Cross an abandoned set of MBTA tracks and continue straight into Memorial Forest, a property of the Sudbury Valley Trustees. At a T-junction (marked H) turn right onto the Desert Loop trail. The path soon skirts a grassy clearing to the right, then re-enters the forest. Close undergrowth gives way to mature pine, along a level trail

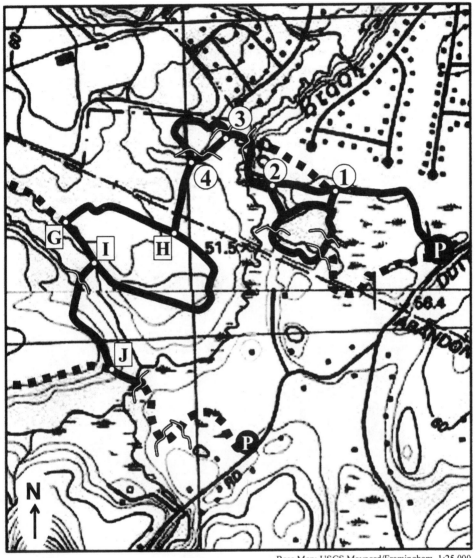

Base Map: USGS Maynard/Framingham 1:25,000

Hop Brook / Memorial Forest, Sudbury

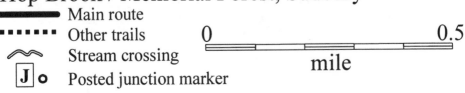

Main route

Other trails

Stream crossing

J ○ Posted junction marker

0   0.5

mile

At a T-junction (G), turn left to continue around the Desert Loop. The path heads downhill. Turn right at the next trail junction (marked I). The trail descends into an area of wetlands surrounding Cranberry Brook. Make your way across the brook via a boardwalk and footbridge, then re-enter the woods. The trail curves through pines, rolling gently up and down.

At junction J, bear left. You will shortly arrive at another bridge crossing lovely Hop Brook and its surrounding wetlands. This is the turnaround point for this suggested hike. (The trail ahead continues to the SVT parking area on Dutton Road via a pine forest subtly decorated with small metal tabs wired to some of the trees. These memorial tags carry the names of women who were members of the nearby Women's Club, hence the name Memorial Forest.)

Hop Brook

Time is but the stream I go a-fishing in. I drink at it; but while I drink, I see the sandy bottom and detect how shallow it is. Its thin current slides away, but eternity remains. I would drink deeper; fish fill the sky, whose bottom is pebbly with stars. I cannot count one. I know not the first letter of the alphabet. I have always been regretting that I was not as wise as the day I was born.

Henry David Thoreau (1817 - 1862)

60

Once you've had your fill of the view, return the way you came, bearing right at junction J and re-crossing Cranberry Brook to junction I. Turn right at I onto the Desert Loop trail. The trail rises slowly, soon curving left and away from the wetland, then leveling into a wide path carpeted with pine needles. After a long straight stretch, you approach the Hop Brook wetlands, and the trail again curves left. After a brief, gentle uphill, bear left over sandy hummocks. The trail skirts a broad sand pit to the right of the path. Bear left away from the sandpit to re-enter the forest. The trail snakes through a gentle S-curve, then straightens. Watch for your return to intersection H, where you turn right, re-crossing the MBTA tracks back into the Hop Brook conservation area via the Marsh-To-Desert Trail.

At a Y-intersection (4), bear left away from your original route, onto the Pitch Pine Trail. The trail winds downhill and across a footbridge over a tributary of Hop Brook. The path then heads uphill again before leveling out amid pine and oak. At a Y-junction, bear right, and right again at a second Y-junction, hiking parallel to the National Wildlife Refuge (NWR) boundary to your left. The trail then winds downhill before leveling out in a wetland area. At a T-junction, turn right (NWR boundary signs are visible to your left) and cross a plank footbridge. At the next junction (3), turn left to rejoin the Marsh-to-Desert Trail.

After you re-cross the Hop Brook footbridge, turn right at the multi-trail junction just across the bridge. Continue to retrace your steps along the sandy, pine needle-strewn path paralleling Hop Brook as the waterway loops sinuously to the right of the trail. After the trail curves away from the brook, bear right at the next trail junction (2), toward Duck Pond. A granite-edged bridge crosses over the pond's spillway to Hop Brook, providing another lovely viewpoint. In sunny spring weather, swarms of snakes have been seen on and around the bridge, basking in the sun and mating.

Across the bridge, continue along the border of the pond, bearing left at a Y-junction and over a boardwalk. The trail continues along the pond's edge. At a T-junction, turn left across a pair of plank boardwalks. You soon see a smaller pond to the right of the trail, asprout with nesting boxes. Cross Duck Pond's feeder stream on a pair of thick timbers (may be flooded in wet season), then bear left at the next Y-junction, following the arrowed Trail signs around the pond. (If the stream is flooded, backtrack to a nearby Y-junction and bear left to the old track-bed; turn left, then take the next left to loop back to the parking area.)

As the trail moves away from the pond through a grove of pines, continue straight, past a yellow Trail arrow pointing to the right. Go straight again as another Trail arrow points left, then turn right (1) on the wide main trail to return to the Hop Brook parking area.

Bridge over Hop Brook

10

Gray Reservation

Town: Sudbury
Rating: Easy (one steep section)
Distance: 1.9 miles
Hiking Time: 1 hour
Maps: USGS Billerica

Summary: This hike involves three interconnected loops of trail, and includes portions of neighboring Haynes Meadow and Pratt's Mill well fields. You will find plenty of variety for hikers of all ages. Ancient glacial features contrast with remnants of the Gray's cabin, dam and pond. Trails twine amidst acres of pines ranging from newly sprouted to immensely mature; much of the way is softly carpeted with their fallen needles. The 1.9 mile route is generally very easy, except for short, steep sections up and down a 40-foot glacial ridge in the well fields area.

Trailhead Location: From I-95/Route 128, follow Route 20 West. At the junction of Routes 20 and 27 in Wayland center, turn right onto Route 27 West toward Sudbury. At the traffic light in Sudbury town center, continue straight on Route 27 for one-quarter mile. Where Route 27 bears right (northwest) at a junction, continue straight (west) on Hudson Road. After another quarter mile, turn left (south) onto Old Lancaster Road. Make an immediate right into an off-road parking area which has room for several cars.

Directions

Begin the hike on a trail just to the right of the Sudbury Valley Trustees kiosk at the parking area. Pass through a small field and into pine and oak woods. After crossing a single-plank bridge and continuing a short distance, turn left at a T-junction (A on map). You are atop a glacial ridge, the first evidence of several types of glacial features on this and the abutting property.

Continue among tall pines studding an under-story of chest-high young ones. Across another, wider plank footbridge, a few short oaks mingle in with the pines as a lower-elevation wetland emerges to your right.

Stay right at a Y-intersection. You soon come to the 'camel's humps' – pine-needle-strewn mounds bordering the wetter area to the right of the trail.

Bear left at the next trail junction after these sandy mounds, but make note of this intersection (B) for a return loop. Take a right at the next junction (C); the trail heads downhill as brushy undergrowth closes in to narrow the pathway.

Another narrow footbridge crosses a small streamlet, which widens out to a shallow pond to your left. You are leaving SVT property as you cross the bridge, moving into the Town of Sudbury's 37-acre Haynes Meadow Conservation Land.

Continue up a brief rise, making note of an arrow-marked trail junction (D), where a path heads off to the left. You will take that path on your return. For now, continue straight ahead to a long, railed bridge over Hop Brook. A cat-tailed marshy area spreads upstream from the bridge, forming a flood plain for the brook. The flow of water riffles over rocks and back into the woods downstream. This is a fine laboratory for young hikers to test the flotation performance of various forest floor objects, and for adults to pause and enjoy the sights and sounds of the active watercourse and its lovely backdrop.

The trail continues along a low glacial ridgeline, with the flood plain to your right and woods to the left. The ridge-top widens out to a pleasant spot for a rest and snack overlooking the marsh. This is your entryway into the Pratts Mill Well Fields of the Sudbury Water District, which includes 3 of the 9 wells managed for the town by the water district. Continue down a short, steep drop to a dry wash and up the other side. A house appears to your left at the junction (E), where a narrow trail dropping off to the right meets the main trail, which continues steeply uphill ahead of you. Take the narrow trail downhill to your right to walk upstream along the edge of the Hop Brook flood plain.

The narrow path slopes along for a few minutes with marsh to the right and the steep glacial ridge climbing up to your left. After the trail levels out and moves away from the marsh and into the woods, note a side trail coming in at a sharp angle from the left. A few paces farther along is another trail junction. Before taking the left branch to continue the loop, detour briefly to your right, to the bank of the brook. Here you find a secluded spot with a lovely view across wetlands and sinuous brook meanderings.

Return to the trail junction, and continue straight across. Pass between two very large pines and bear left to climb steeply up the ridge, leaving a metal boundary post and a small, fenced-in utility building to your right.

Pause at the top to consider that you have just climbed up the 40-foot ice-contact face pushed ahead of a glacier long ago. In front of you is a kame plain, deposited by glacial melt water and pitted with kettle holes.

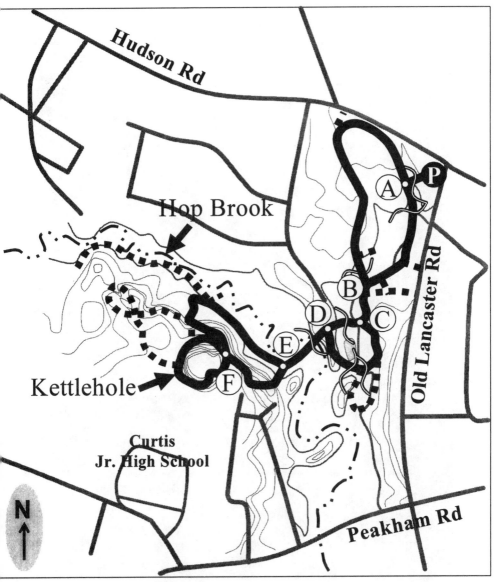

Hudson Rd

Hop Brook

(A) :(P)

Old Lancaster Rd

(B)

(D) (C)

Kettlehole
(E)

(F)

Curtis
Jr. High School

N

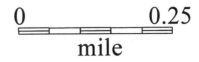

Peakham Rd

Base Map: USGS Billerica 1:25,000

Gray Reservation, Sudbury

——— Main route
▪▪▪▪▪▪ Other trails
〜 Stream crossing

0   0.25

mile

Pond View

Turn left at the trail junction at the top of the ridge. Enjoy the steep drop-away to your left and the view across the Hop Brook flood plain you earlier skirted just above water level.

At a multiple trail intersection (F) just past the narrowest part of the ridge, take another detour from the loop by bearing right to the middle of the three trails available. This path drops steeply down into an enormous kettle hole that harbors a sphagnum bog at its low point. Continue left and steeply up for a higher-level look across the kettle hole at the narrow ridge you just crossed. Follow the trail as it loops around the top of the kettlehole, past various side trails and back to junction F. Here, take the second trail to the right as you face the Hop Brook flood plain. The ridge-top soon narrows, with another kettle hole dropping off to your right.

Bear left at the next Y-junction, away from a paved road visible through the trees. Head carefully along the very steep trail slicing downhill from the top of the glacial ridge. The trail levels out as you re-encounter intersection E, completing the loop through Water District property. Continue straight ahead to return to the long railed bridge over Hop Brook.

After re-crossing the bridge, take the second right at a marked trail junction (D on map), avoiding an earlier, unmarked side trail a few paces closer to the brook behind you. You are again on the Town of Sudbury's Haynes Meadow Conservation Land.

Stroll gently down-slope through pine and oak to a smaller railed footbridge, built as an Eagle Scout project. A trickle of water drains the shallow pond to your left, even during fairly dry periods.

Bear left at the next trail junction, dipping down across a single-board bridge to an immediate T-junction where you again turn left. At the next junction (C) bear right, returning to an earlier part of your hike.

At the next Y-junction (B) bear left, away from your original route and across a plank bridge over a gap in a concrete and stone dam. To create the pond, the dam was built into a natural glacial esker by Stephen Gray. A few paces ahead are a stone fireplace and chimney; these are all that remains of the Gray's cabin. Continue ahead, leaving the chimney to your left. (If you stroll along this trail in winter, you may see evidence of deer having stripped bark from young pines for winter food.) After a few more minutes, bear right at a Y and enter an area of much older and larger pines.

Bear right again at yet another Y-junction, curving away from the sound of nearby Hudson Road. Continuing on the trail through the pines, you pass a stone fence to your left, and then an enormous multi-trunk pine on the right. After heading up a short steep rise to the crest of a glacial ridge, watch for the next trail to your left (A), and follow it back to the parking area.

Hop Brook wetland hemmed in by glacial ridges

I encounter other people only occasionally while walking these trails, and hiking early on a weekend morning reduces the likelihood even further. I find an added pleasure in the tickling of gossamer strands spun by spiders overnight. They try but fail to capture me in their delicate, sticky grasp: I'm the first to pass this way today!
- Notes from author's journal

11

Weir Hill / Round Hill

Town: Sudbury
Rating: Moderate
Distance: 2.1 miles
Hiking Time: 1 - 1.5 hour
Maps: USGS Maynard

Summary: Weir Hill's fascinating glacial features, lovely views of the Sudbury River, plus the higher perspective from the open summit of neighboring Round Hill, add up to a spectacular hike. This 2.1-mile route is easy except for a few minutes' moderately steep climb to the top of each of the two hills.

Trailhead Location: From the light at the junction of Concord Road and Old Sudbury Road (Route 27) in Sudbury, drive north on Concord, turning right onto Lincoln Road after 1.1 miles. Turn onto Weir Hill Road, which is on your left after 1.3 miles. The suggested hike below begins from a parking area at the northern end of Weir Hill Road. Parking is also available at Lincoln Meadows on Lincoln Road west of Weir Hill Road, or at Refuge Headquarters on Weir Hill Road, but the gate across the access road to the headquarters building is sometimes closed.

Directions

From the parking area on Weir Hill Road, cross the street and head past the trailhead kiosk, uphill along a wood-bordered path and steps snaking up the steep slope. At the top, a tree-filtered view to the west provides a hint of the beauty ahead.

The now-level trail continues to skirt the steep drop-off marking the edge of the kame plain. Shortly after you pass a bench, the trail eases away from the edge to pass by a kettle hole. An explanatory placard describes how Weir Hill was formed at the edge of a retreating glacier.

A short distance beyond the kettle hole, the trail returns to the edge of the steep slope to overlook the Sudbury River beyond. Another bench is well placed for enjoying the view.

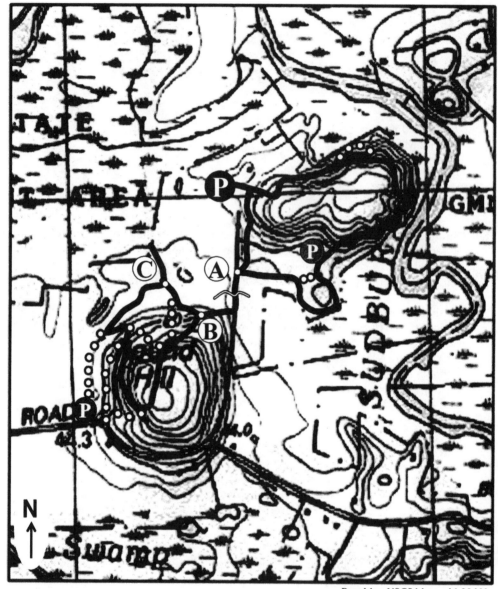

Weir Hill / Round Hill, Sudbury

▬▬▬	Main route
ooooo	Other trails
〰	Stream crossing

Base Map: USGS Maynard 1:25,000

0   0.5

mile

Continue to follow the yellow trail markers to arrive at an even more striking view of the winding river stretching off to the east. Another wood-bordered path and step section helps in traversing the steep down-slope, taking you to the river's edge and the most ideally sited bench of all, overlooking the serene river and its surrounding wetlands. A concrete boat ramp provides easy access for visitors arriving from the river.

After you have absorbed your fill of the beauty of this spot, continue along the wide and level path, paralleling the river for a while before its rightward curve leads you to the visitor's center and its parking area. Follow the paved access road ahead until the loop trail strikes off to the left, just before the main visitor parking area. Continue on the trail toward a pond, then bear left to circle the pond on a narrow strip of land separating it from the river proper. At a T-junction past the pond, turn left and continue past a large shelter.

The next trail junction (intersection A on map) lies just past a placard for a red maple tree. Turn left, crossing two footbridges on your way to Weir Hill Road. Continue across the road to Intersection B, where you turn left. The trail continues uphill among tall pines, including many very mature specimens. The uphill climb is steady and moderately steep. Shortly a trail comes in from the right. Continue straight and uphill.

At a T-junction, turn left, continuing uphill through an area dominated by pine but with some oak mixed in as well. You soon pass over a stone fence, and the slope eases as you arrive at a hilltop clearing. Continue ahead to the far side of the clearing to enjoy the fine view. A well-placed granite bench is waiting for you just before a low stone fence. This is a fall concentration spot for bird migrants. Under ideal conditions significant numbers of hawks pass by the summit of the hill.

When you have enjoyed the view to the fullest and are ready to descend, continue alongside the stone fence on your original path across the meadow, leaving a lone cedar tree to your left. The trail curves into mixed evergreen and deciduous, including oak, birch, cedar and pine, on a gentle down-slope.

Pass by one trail to your left and then, at a T-junction partway around the hill, turn left. Take the next trail to your right, passing through a border of cut tree trunk segments lining the wide path. This narrow trail continues downhill through a low muddy spot, then turns right, becoming more overgrown, but still passable. The trail angles left, still on the level, then curves to the right toward a small pond partially hidden behind a screen of trees and undergrowth. At a Y-intersection by the pond's edge (C on map), you may choose to take a brief detour to the left, to the boundary of the wildlife management area around the nearby Sudbury River, for a sweeping ground-level view of the wetlands.

To continue with the main hike, bear right at the junction by the pond. The trail is slightly uphill, leading through another muddy spot and into tall pines, where the upslope becomes a bit steeper. At a T-junction with a Sudbury Valley Trustees trail marker, turn left as the arrow indicates. The trail curves across the flank of the hill among the scent of pines.

Double-crested cormorant

Sudbury River at Weir Hill Landing

At the next trail junction (B) turn left. The trail leads downhill, then levels as you retrace your original route across Weir Hill Road. Upon returning over the footbridges to A, continue straight. You will soon cross the access road for the refuge's Visitor Center, then head uphill on a moderate slope. At a trail junction above the parking area from which you set out, turn left and downhill to finish your hike.

> Climb the mountains and get their good tidings. Nature's peace will flow into you as sunshine flows into trees. The winds will blow their own freshness into you, and the storms their energy, while cares will drop away from you like the leaves of Autumn.
>
> John Muir (1838 - 1914)

12

Mount Misery / Farrar Pond

Town: Lincoln
Rating: Moderate
Distance: 5.0 miles
Hiking Time: 2 - 3 hours
Maps: USGS Maynard

Summary: This hike combines the popular routes around Mount Misery with the more secluded trail tracing Farrar Pond's shoreline, resulting in a 5-mile leg stretcher. Enjoy Beaver Dam Brook's chain of ponds before scaling Mount Misery, then circle a kettlehole pond on your way to the banks of the Sudbury River. Lovely Farrar Pond awaits you on the south side of Route 117; the pond is seen by many travellers on this busy road but circled by few.

Trailhead Location: From the junction of 117 and 126 in Lincoln, the main parking area lies 0.7 miles to the west, on the north side of the street. Parking is also available another 0.3 miles east, at the canoe landing.

Directions

From the main parking lot, head east past the kiosk to the edge of a large pond. Turn right, following the path around the pond, past a set of steps leading up to Route 117. The trail rolls very gently under a carpet of pine needles. Continue straight at a Y-junction to a T-junction with a bridge to the left. This and other bridges along Beaver Dam Brook have lovely curving stonework.

Turn right at the T, heading uphill, then bear left at a multi-trail junction to walk parallel to the brook. The water rushes noisily to your left, over a beaver dam and past an old mill site. At the next junction, continue straight alongside another, smaller pond, then bear left at a Y-junction as the trail eases downhill and across another bridge over Beaver Dam Brook (A on map).

Just across the bridge, bear left, heading uphill on a narrower trail. Continue straight as a trail comes in from your right, through a grove of hemlocks to a 4-way intersection. Bear right to ascend to Mount Misery's 265 foot summit.

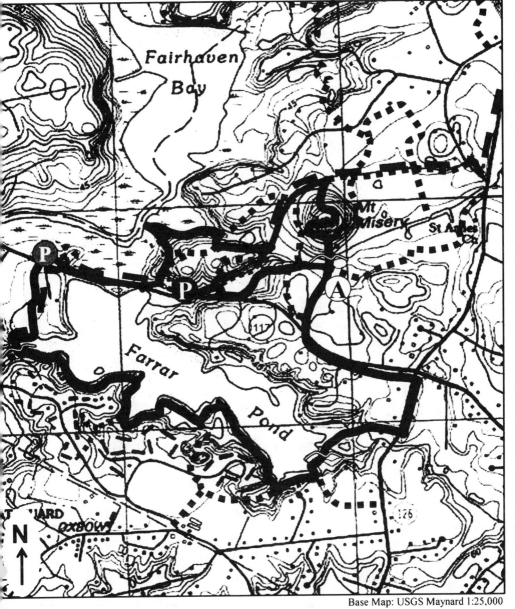

Mount Misery / Farrar Pond, Lincoln

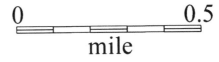

━━━━ Main route
▪▪▪▪▪▪▪ Other trails
∿∿ Stream crossing
━ ━ Bay Circuit Trail

Base Map: USGS Maynard 1:25,000

0   0.5
mile

The yellow-marked trail winds uphill. At the top, detour left at a T-junction to an overlook for a narrow view to the southeast before continuing to the right down the north slope. This wider trail has a gentler slope than the ascent, and it leads you to an even broader main trail; turn left. You are now on the Bay Circuit Trail.

Continue across a 4-way intersection. After a gentle down-slope, the trail levels before a Y-junction; turn right and uphill. Terrapin Lake nestles downhill to your right. The trail levels at the top of the broad ridge separating Terrapin Lake from the largest of the Beaver Dam Brook's ponds.

Turn right and downhill at the next junction. Terrapin Lake still glistens to your right. Continue straight at the next two intersections, staying on the "Kettle" Trail. ("Kettle" is short for Kettlehole, describing the origin of Terrapin Lake in the glacial era.) The wide, needle-strewn path rolls easily alongside the wetlands of the Sudbury River to your right.

At the next junction, continue straight; the trail narrows. Take a right at the next T-junction to arrive at the edge of the Sudbury at Knacker's Point. A lovely view of the river greets you. In times of lower water, you can see where flood-level waters have painted bands of discoloration on the vegetation across the way.

When you've had your fill of the river view, head straight away from the water and uphill, continuing straight through two nearby trail junctions. Bear right at a wide Y, still on the Kettle Trail heading uphill. At the crest continue straight again as a trail heads left. The next Y-junction offers you the chance to turn left and regain the parking lot; however, this hike continues to the right, toward Farrar's Pond.

The trail curves downhill to the right to run between Route 117 and the Sudbury River's wetlands. The trail soon rises up again to the canoe landing parking lot; walk to the far end, then cross Route 117 and turn right (west) toward a driveway serving several houses. Turn left into the driveway, noticing the Bay Circuit Trail marker on the trail post at the edge of the road.

Follow the driveway, turning right at the fork, then watch for another trail post on the left. Turn left onto the grassy path threading between two fence lines. Follow the left-hand fence downhill. The trail curves to the right at the end of the fence to run along the edge of the pond.

Island in Farrar Pond

The trail soon turns left to cross a narrow footbridge over outflow pipes and a spillway, designed to prevent beaver blockage. Across the bridge, bear left past two side trails and continue around the pond. The trail follows the shoreline, climbing up a ridge, then running across its steeply-sloping face. The narrow trail requires some attention, but the challenge is more than compensated by the lovely view of the pond and a nearby tree-covered island.

After a sharp dip and rise, the trail leads to a T-junction. Detour left, out onto a small point decorated by birches, for a closer perspective on the pond, then head away from the water and uphill. The trail continues up and down the ridge face. Past a level spot where a variety of boats are stored, turn left to continue around the pond. At the next T, detour left again for another view, then continue right through a blueberry thicket.

The trail runs along a shallower hillside below several houses. At a T-junction by a tiny inlet, turn left. The trail then cuts very close to the shore by a low-lying island before returning to a narrow course along a steep ridge face. As the trail nears the head of the pond and goes up a short, steep slope, turn left at the T–junction, then bear right past a small shack and boats. The trail crosses a double-tracked grassy lane in a small meadow, then descends through a swampy area to emerge at the base of a private yard.

Follow a series of fence-lines ahead to an unpaved driveway, and turn right to arrive at Route 126. Cross the road, then turn left and follow the sidewalk to the lights at the junction of 126 and 117. In spring, flowering trees and bushes provide color and scent along the way. Turn left again at the light and take the sidewalk along the south side of 117, heading west.

While the sidewalk will eventually lead you to the wooden stairs by the large pond and the parking lot, you may want a quieter route. If so, watch for a green-painted metal post on the north side of the street, just east of the driveway to #99. Cross the road and head back into the woods. Turn left before the footbridge (A) and retrace your steps along the south side of Beaver Dam Brook and its ponds to return to the parking area.

Below: View from Mount Misery   *Facing page: Delaney Reservoir, Harvard (Hike # 18)*

Assabet River Watershed

13

Headwaters Conservation Area

Town: Westborough
Rating: Moderate
Distance: 1.7 miles
Hiking Time: 45 min. - 1 hour
Maps: USGS Marlborough

Summary: Westborough's Charm Bracelet (WCB) trail system includes the source of the Assabet River -- the SuAsCo (Nichols) Reservoir. The 120-acre Headwaters Conservation Area encompasses the wooded heights of Oak Ridge as well as fine views from the trailhead kiosk and at Osprey Point along the shoreline. In spring, you will find vernal pools; in summertime, a butterfly garden provides additional interest. Trails are generally easy, with occasional steeper sections. A 1.7-mile route is suggested here, but you can extend your exploration along the interior network of trails; you may also follow the WCB trail east along the reservoir.

Trailhead Location: Head west on Route 30 (West Main Street) from the rotary in the center of Westborough. Bear right after 1.3 miles onto Nourse Street, then right again onto Old Nourse. After 0.4 mile, turn right onto Andrews Street, and drive to the far end. There is room for several cars to park on the left, before a gate across the road.

Directions

Head north from the parking area, to the left of the gate. You are immediately rewarded with a fine view across the reservoir toward Boston Hill, which rises steeply to over 560 feet. Continue past the kiosk on a wide trail downhill. You'll pass a sign (A on map) indicating that you are headed toward Osprey Point; the Oak Ridge Trail runs uphill to your left.

Continue into the woods toward Osprey Point, passing additional signed trails to your left. After 0.2 mile, a path coming in from the right, bringing with it the markers of the Westborough Charm Bracelet trail system, which extends throughout the town.

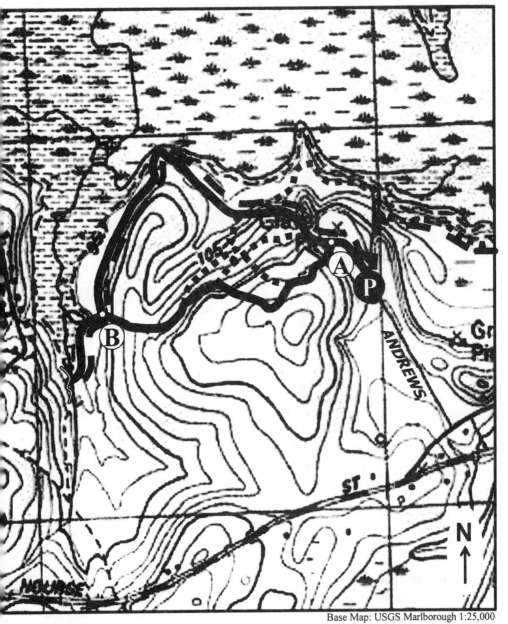

Base Map: USGS Marlborough 1:25,000

Headwaters, Westborough

▬▬▬▬	Main route
▪▪▪▪▪▪	Other trails
∿∿	Stream crossing
▬ ▬ ▬	Westborough Charm Bracelet Trail

0   0.5

mile

Heron and osprey nests at Osprey Point

Bear right at a Y-junction, continuing toward Osprey Point. Where you meet the Eagle Trail, pause to make your way to the right. At the water's edge you will be rewarded with a sweeping view across the reservoir, punctuated by dead tree trunks sprinkled with blue heron and osprey nests.

Head away from the water on the Eagle Trail, now bound for what the local scouts' signs tell you is the Assabet River. The trail weaves between the hill to your left and the reservoir's wetland on the right. Continue straight past a sign pointing left to Oak Ridge (B), passing along a narrow boardwalk to a bridge over the wide stream of the Assabet. After enjoying its vigorously rushing flow, retrace your steps to B and turn right to climb Oak Ridge.

You'll ascend about 100 feet, not quite achieving the highest local elevation, which lies off the trail to the south. To stay on the Oak Ridge Trail, bear right at a signed Y-junction with the Middle Branch trail, and right again nearer the summit, at a T-junction with a cut-off trail. Several unsigned trails also lead right, toward a nearby school. As the trail starts to head downhill again, stay right at another signed junction with the Middle Branch Trail. The trail drops more steeply now, following switchbacks down to the wide main trail at A. Turn right to return to the parking area.

14

Garfield Woods / Forty Caves

Town: Berlin
Rating: Moderate
Distance: 2.3 miles, plus 1.2 mile extension
Hiking Time: 1 - 2 hours
Maps: USGS Hudson

Summary: Garfield Woods has much to offer visitors. North Brook flows through riffles, slides under slabs of rock, and slows to form still pools on its way to the Assabet River. Children love to explore the brook's every feature in great detail, and to climb over and among the many boulders and outcroppings throughout the area. The main trail follows the stream bank, then winds among dramatic rock outcroppings and above ravines. An additional loop extends the hike into Berlin conservation land. This tour of the property covers 2.3 miles of trail over terrain of moderate difficulty, including a few briefly steep sections. The extension into Musche Woods adds 1.2 miles.

Trailhead Location: From I-195, drive 3.2 miles west from on Route 62. Just after crossing a set of railroad tracks, turn right, then after ¼ mile, turn right again onto Randall Road. After 0.7 mile, bear left at a Y-junction onto Lancaster Road. The Sudbury Valley Trustees trailhead sign is located on the west side of Lancaster Road, 0.7 miles north of the junction of Lancaster and Randall. Ample parking is available along the wide flat shoulder.

Directions

From Lancaster Road, the trail leads westward past an SVT kiosk. North Brook burbles in from the right to parallel the path before passing under the Conrail tracks. Walk to the right alongside the tracks to cross the brook, then cross the tracks to your left to continue hiking into the woods. *CAUTION:* these tracks are active!

A few paces away from the tracks, the brook turns abruptly left at a massive granite outcropping. Just ahead, over a short boardwalk, is a trail junction (A on map). Turn left onto the main trail for this property, marked with blue triangles.

Base Map: USGS Hudson 1:25,000

Garfield Woods / Forty Caves, Berlin

	Main route
	Extension
	Other trails
	Stream crossing

0   0.5
mile

The trail passes across two more boardwalks, then continues parallel to North Brook. The brook flows over and under massive granite boulders, providing a constant backdrop of gurgling sound as it goes. Note the yellow-blazed trail that heads off to the right (B); you will return to this point later.

Continue ahead on the blue trail as it turns away from the brook and crosses a stone fence onto Berlin Conservation Commission Land (the Forty Caves area). After crossing a streamlet, the trail angles away from the brook and uphill into a quiet area of forest.

Just after the red trail comes in from the right, turn left at C onto an un-blazed trail. The trail heads uphill but soon levels off. Bear left at junction D. A ravine drops away to the right of the trail. You may detour right onto one of several short side trails for a view into its depths. The main trail eventually curves downhill to the railroad tracks; turn around and retrace your steps.

Back at junction D, bear left to continue alongside the ravine before returning to the blue trail at junction E. Turn right, then take an immediate left at C, heading uphill on a narrow, red-blazed trail. The trail curves around massive outcrops and boulders. To the right looms a large granite ridge. At junction F, turn right, then almost immediately right again at G onto the yellow-blazed trail.

A brief, moderately steep climb brings you to the crest of the granite ridge you passed earlier. Along the way you'll find many fine spots for a rest break. The trail continues to wind closely among boulders toward the growing sound of North Brook's rushing waters. You rejoin the blue trail at junction B. Turn left, retracing your steps to junction A. At junction A, bear left to continue around the perimeter of the property.

Head northeast, away from North Brook, with the railroad tracks to your right. Follow the blue trail parallel to the tracks. It soon bears left, away from the tracks. Pass by junctions G (yellow trail) and F (red trail), continuing straight on blue. (Just after F, at J, the optional trail heads right, into Musche Woods.) As the trail reaches a point where it is about to plunge very steeply downhill, turn left onto the white-blazed trail (junction H). (Going straight takes you into Musche Woods.) As you go downhill, enjoy the down-slope view over a nearby stone fence and a streamlet beyond, to a distant horizon through the trees.

At the low point of the trail, the stream comes in from the right to parallel your path just before a trail junction (I). Another stream can be seen crossing the path farther to your right; the two will soon join North Brook. After enjoying the gurgle from water flowing over rocks, head left at junction I. The way trends uphill as the waterway disappears to your right, with more fine outcroppings to the left. You return quickly to junction E, then C, and continue along North Brook past B and over the two boardwalk segments to junction A. Turn right here and re-cross the railroad tracks toward Lancaster Road and the trailhead.

15

Edmund Hill

Town: Northborough
Rating: Moderate
Distance: 2.0 miles
Hiking Time: 45 min. - 1 hour
Maps: Marlborough

Summary: Wetlands, pine forest and hilltop combine at Edmund Hill, a pocket of conservation land nestled near residential neighborhoods and a railway just north of the Assabet. Handmade signs naming the trails for various birds enliven the 2-mile double-loop route.

Trailhead Location: From Route 20 in the center of Northborough, follow Hudson Street northeast about 0.9 mile. Turn left onto Allen Street, then continue across its junction with Rice Avenue to the parking area for Edmund Hill. The off-road lot has room for several cars.

Directions

From the parking area, the red-blazed main trail heads northwest, threading among hillocks and along a low ridge. At a junction marked by a post and a blue triangle (A on map), turn left. This narrower path leads alongside a cattailed pond, then turns right at another post to descend into the heart of the wetland. The stream you soon cross has a mere half-mile remaining before it empties into the Assabet River. The blue trail continues through the wetlands before rising to dry ground beneath an extensive grove of tall pines. What a contrast in habitat, attained in just a few strides!

Follow the blue markers to a four-way intersection just east of the railroad tracks, and then turn right, continuing on blue. The blue trail ends at another four-way junction with the red and yellow trails (B). If you continued straight on the red Summit Trail you would go directly to the top of Edmund Hill, but I recommend turning left on the Goldfinch trail (yellow markers). This path weaves along the base of the hill, paralleling the tracks, for 0.4 mile before emerging at the edge of a pond at the town's Colburn Street recreation facility.

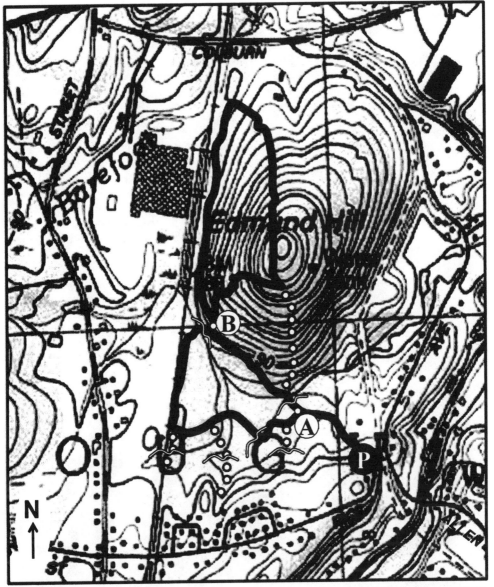

Base Map: USGS Marlborough 1:25,000

Edmund Hill, Northborough

▬▬▬▬	Main route
oooo	Other trails
∿∿	Stream crossing

0   0.5

mile

Turn right alongside the pond, and head uphill toward a line of vertical posts running alongside a dirt road. Pass by a lone cedar tree and re-enter the woods to the left of a metal gate, by a small trail sign. You are now on your way to the 441-foot summit of Edmund Hill, an ascent of about 160 feet in 0.3 miles. Near the top, you will see the bald pate of a water tank peeking over the crest of the hill to your left. Though the summit is wooded, there is little undergrowth to interfere with a real sense of altitude.

Just past the summit, your trail arrives at a T-junction with the red-marked Cardinal Trail. While you may descend either to the left or the right, I like the right-hand path as it takes you along the margin between hillside and wetland on its way back to the parking area. If you do turn right at this juncture, you will descend Edmund Hill to a familiar four-way junction with the yellow and blue trails (B); turn left on red. The trail runs around the base of the hill with wetland to your right. At a Y-junction with the other arm of the red trail, turn right. The trail passes over the same stream once more before returning through junction A to the parking area.

> *Finally, a sunny day in early spring after a long, cold, snowy winter!*
> *Bird-song has returned to the woods, and so has a ribbon snake,*
> *draped elegantly across the trail to take advantage of a puddle of light.*
> *As I halt to take a look, I notice movement out of the corner of my eye,*
> *hear a gentle rasping-rustling sound – and lose interest in the solo*
> *snake. A half-dozen more are writhing nearby in their early-spring*
> *mating ritual. They pause but do not scatter, merely watching me*
> *watch them. I step away and the ritual continues.*
> – Notes from author's journal

Eastern ribbon snakes (Thamnophis sauitus) in spring

16

Danforth Falls

Town: Hudson
Rating: Moderate
Distance: 1.7 miles
Hiking Time: 45 min. - 1 hour
Maps: USGS Hudson

Summary: A 1.7 mile exploration along Danforth Brook and to the top of Phillips Hill, which offers a wide view to the west. The brook spills over Danforth Falls, the highest waterfall in the Assabet River watershed at 20-25 feet. You will encounter some steep sections while ascending Phillips Hill.

Trailhead Location: The Danforth Lot is on the west side of Route 85 (Lincoln Street) in Hudson, 0.9 miles north of the traffic circle at the junction of 62 and 85 in the center of town. The roadside parking area has room for two cars.

Directions

Enter past a metal gate just north of the parking area. Follow the wide, level trail parallel to Danforth Brook on the right. Continue straight at A as two trails branch off to the left. After a brief, moderately steep climb, bear right on a wide trail (B). Continue straight as a narrow trail crosses the main trail on a diagonal.

Across the brook to your right, huge granite outcrops emerge as you approach the falls. Where the main trail turns left (to private property) at a pond above the falls, continue straight a few steps more for a view out over the water, then return down the main trail to B.

Continue straight at B on the wide trail, then bear right at C past a circle of stones. Just after ducking under a large tree lying across the trail, notice a stone structure to the right of the trail. Shortly thereafter, where a section of stone fence runs parallel to the trail on the left, and the trunk of a pine tree to the left of the trail curves in an "S", turn right (D). The trail soon heads uphill, moderately steeply, then leveling out as you approach the summit of Phillips Hill.

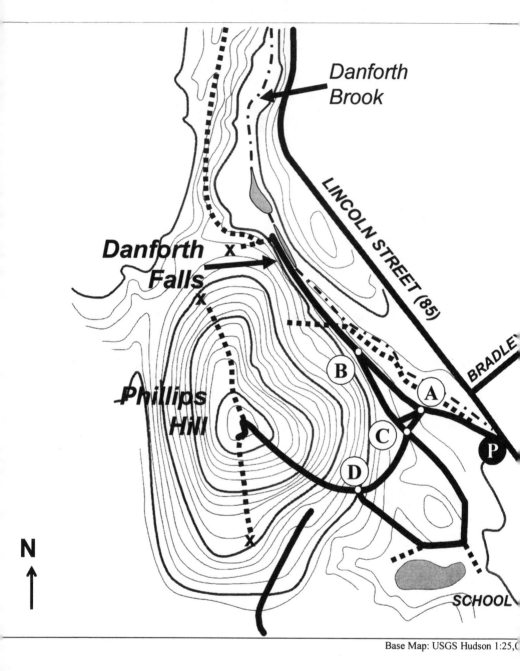

Danforth Brook

LINCOLN STREET (85)

BRADLEY

Danforth Falls

x

x

Phillips Hill

B

A

C

D

P

x

SCHOOL

Base Map: USGS Hudson 1:25,0

N

Danforth Falls, Hudson

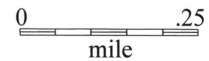

—————— Main route
▪▪▪▪▪▪▪▪ Other trails

0   .25
mile

For a fine view in a westerly direction from the summit, take a sharp left in the clearing at the top of the hill, then bear right just before a boulder with a short metal post sticking out of it.

When you are ready, descend Phillips Hill to D, then turn right to loop through a low-lying area behind the C. A. Farley School. At a T-junction by a pond, turn left, then left again at the far end of the pond, nearest the school. The trail leads atop what in the 1870s was built to be a bed for the Hudson and Lancaster Railroad. At the far end of the ridgeline, the trail drops back down to junction C. Turn right, and right again at A, to return to the trailhead.

Danforth Falls

17

Great Elms / Williams Pond

Town: Harvard
Rating: Moderate
Distance: 2.5 miles
Hiking Time: 1 - 1.5 hours
Maps: USGS Hudson

Summary: Two adjoining parcels in southeast Harvard offer you a moderate ramble past a lovely pond and through forested uplands strewn in places with a variety of gigantic boulders. Enjoy an open field laced with a stream; another stream runs along the base of a steep, rocky hill – Be prepared for a few briefly steep sections of trail here. The suggested route totals 2.5 miles.

Trailhead Location: From the junction of I-495 / Route 111 in Boxborough, drive west on Route 111 for 1.7 miles, then take a sharp left onto Stow Road. Follow Stow Road for 0.7 mile to the corner of Stow Road and Murray's Lane in Harvard. Park in the small pull-off by Williams Pond, located on the north side of Stow Road.

Directions

From the parking area, head north along the eastern shore of the pond. Your way is marked by yellow blazes. At the far end of the pond, continue straight at a trail junction (A on map), heading uphill into an area studded with striking glacial erratics – enormous boulders deposited thousands of years ago.

At a Y-junction, bear left onto a blue-blazed trail, then left again at another Y. The trail heads briefly downhill, over a stone fence and across a small stream, then circles to the left around a beautiful open field with a large granite outcrop at its crest.

As you round the outcrop and bear right across the top of the meadow, watch for a narrow trail heading left in the far corner, and follow it back into the woods. Bear left at the junction with the yellow trail.

When you arrive at a T-junction (B), turn left. The area ahead may be quite wet; you can skirt it by circling left through the underbrush to the stone fence on the far side. The trail passes through a small gap in the fence, and on to another vast meadow, where the path turns right to head downhill.

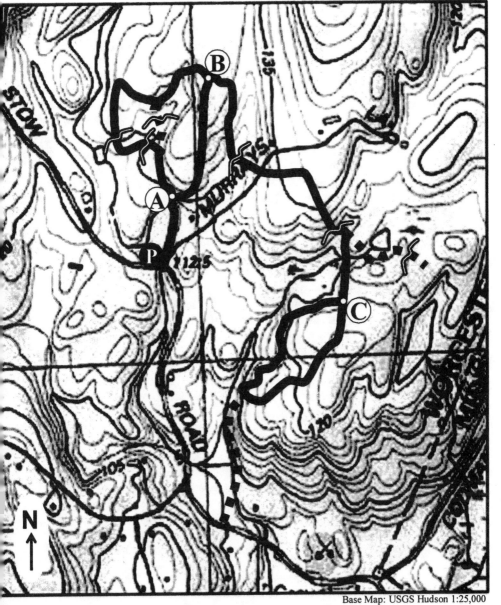

Great Elms / Williams Pond, Harvard

——— Main route
■■■■■ Other trails
∼∼ Stream crossing

0   0.5

mile

Base Map: USGS Hudson 1:25,000

At the base of the field, step across a stream, which is on its way to nearby Elizabeth Brook. The trail takes you briefly uphill to Murray's Lane. Continue across the pavement onto a narrow easement trail running uphill between private parcels. The trail climbs on a moderate slope, then descends more steeply to the south before crossing a small stream. As you ascend the slope on the far side of the stream, you may wish to detour left on a birdwatcher's path to a small pond.

Continuing on the main trail, turn right in less than a tenth of a mile at a well-blazed junction (C). This segment of trail takes you past a boggy wetland and along the stream draining it. The trail eventually descends on a moderate slope to a trail junction near the rushing stream, where the main trail takes a sharp turn uphill to the left. (You may wish to continue downstream for a bit, on a somewhat challenging path threading between the stream and the steep hill to your left – a lovely stretch.)

Make your way up the moderately steep slope, heading away from the stream. You will close this loop in about a quarter-mile at C. Retrace your path to Murray's Lane. Here, you may turn left along the lane to return easily to the parking area a quarter-mile away; however the recommended route continues back across the lane and stream, and back up the field to the trail junction on the far side of the stone fence. At this intersection, continue straight, now on a segment of trail you have not yet trodden.

The path heads easily downhill, past more fine boulders, returning you to the northern end of Williams Pond at junction A. Bear left to return along the pond to the parking area.

Aural encounters in the woods can be even more thrilling than spotting your fellow creatures, in the first moment of "What was that?!". The rattle and whoosh of the great blue heron departing long before the camera is ready, the gallop of unseen deer startled from their daybeds, the whistling flight of a flock of mourning doves, a scavenging crow or squirrel sounding much larger than life as it picks through the leafy carpet in search of edible morsels – all provide brief crescendos of excitement against the steady background murmur of breeze-stirred rustlings, avian twitters, and the crunch of your own footsteps.
                                            - Notes from author's journal

Williams Pond

Such an ocean of wooded, waving, swelling mountain beauty and
grandeur is not to be described. Countless forest-clad hills, side by side
in rows and groups, seemed to be enjoying the rich sunshine and
remaining motionless only because they were so eagerly absorbing it.
All were united by curves and slope of inimitable softness and beauty.
O these forest gardens of our Father! What perfection, what divinity, in
their architecture! What simplicity and mysterious complexity of
detail! Who shall read the teaching of these sylvan pages, the glad
brotherhood of rills that sing in the valley, and all the happy creatures
that dwell in them under the tender keeping of a Father's care?
John Muir, *A Thousand Mile Walk to the Gulf*

18

Delaney Project

Town: Harvard
Rating: Moderate
Distance: 4.4 miles
Hiking Time: 2 - 3 hours
Maps: USGS Hudson

Summary: A pair of hikes totaling 4.4 miles, passing through woodland, meadow and wetland habitats, and offering a corresponding variety of flora and fauna, including lady slippers and blackberries, turtles and snakes sunning themselves, and great blue herons fishing or gliding overhead. The suggested routes include several short, steep climbs up and down glacial ridges, as well as some muddy spots.

Trailhead Location: From the light at the junction of 117 and 62 in Stow, drive west on 117; turn right after one mile onto Harvard Road. Follow Harvard Road for 2.1 miles, past the Delaney boat ramp parking area; turn left onto Harvard Road, which becomes Finn Road just west of the Harvard-Stow border. The suggested hikes below start from roadside parking for several cars on both sides of Finn Road, 0.3 miles west of Harvard Road.

CAUTION

Hunting is permitted on the Delaney project. The hunting season runs approximately October to December. Wear bright orange clothing for safety.

Directions - North Parcel

Head north from the parking area, continuing straight as a trail heads off to the right. At the next trail junction (A on map) continue straight, staying on the ridge, with forested wetlands on both sides. Turn right at B as the trail climbs slightly. At a T-junction (C), turn left onto a wide, level trail.

At the next junction (D) turn right, descending from the ridge on a moderately steep slope. The trail soon levels and becomes occasionally muddy as you skirt a wetland, with a fine view to the left over the lush marsh grasses.

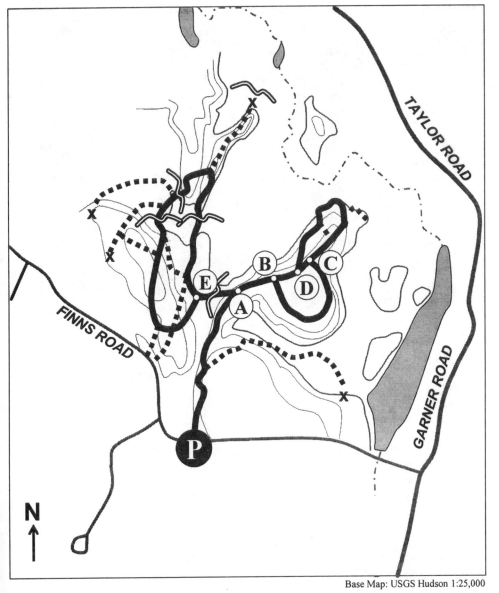

TAYLOR ROAD

FINNS ROAD

GARNER ROAD

B

C

E

A

D

P

N

Base Map: USGS Hudson 1:25,000

Delaney North, Harvard

———— Main route
▪▪▪▪▪▪▪ Other trails
〰〰 Stream crossing

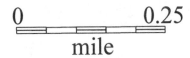

0   0.25
mile

View across water

Several trails converge at a lovely spot by the edge of an open pond, decorated with yellow-flowering lily pads, Continue ahead, parallel to the water, bearing left at a Y-junction. You'll pass a beaver lodge on the left, and the remains of an old chimney on your right.

The trail soon curves sharply right and uphill away from the water. Turn right at a T-junction, and continue straight past junctions C, D and B. At junction A, turn right on a wide path and descend on a moderate slope. The trail soon levels at a low spot between wetlands.

Continue straight at a trail junction (E), heading uphill on a moderately steep slope; turn right at a T-junction onto the ridge-top path. At a Y-junction, bear right and descend from the ridgeline. Make your way across a burbling stream on a fallen tree trunk – a walking stick is very helpful here!

Head uphill and along another ridge-top trail. Soon the trail dips moderately steeply to angle down the ridge to the left into dense forest. Turn left at a Y-junction at the foot of the slope, then continue straight as another trail comes in from the right.

A rough wooden bridge carries you across a deeply-cut stream. Just on the other side of the bridge, turn left. The path parallels the stream for a time, then heads uphill on a moderate slope. Just as it begins to rise, bear right at a Y-junction, continuing uphill. At the top, continue straight as a trail angles in from the right. Bear left at a multi-trail junction; continue to bear left at a series of trail junctions, heading downhill.

Go straight at a Y-junction just past the wet area. Back at E, turn right, then right again and uphill at a Y-junction. Turn right again at the top of the ridge (A) to return to the parking area.

Stream below Delaney dam

Directions – South Parcel

From the west end of the Finn Road parking area, walk past a metal gate. Continue on the main trail after it levels, as other trails head off to either side. As a trail comes in from the left, bear right (Intersection A on map). Bear left at a Y-junction (B), following a narrow trail across an open meadow. After passing a stone fence, bear right and downhill at a Y-junction (C), heading back into the woods. Cross a stream draining one wetland area into another, noting the dramatic habitat change. Past another stone fence, you head into another open meadow. As the undergrowth closes in to narrow the meadow, continue straight at a Y-junction (D). As you cross a stone fence gap to another junction, continue straight into another open area. Continue straight at E, dropping steeply down into a wide channel, across a stream, then up the other side.

The trail ahead carries you past F and on to the Delaney floodplain, again dropping steeply down hill. Continue past G straight across toward the dam, climbing up its embankment to H. Enjoy the wide-ranging view from the top of the dam (a superb spot for winter sledding), then head northwest, down off the embankment and along the water's edge. The original purpose of the project was waterfowl management, to include hunting, as well as flood control on Elizabeth Brook. The brook is the largest tributary of the Assabet River, which in turn is the largest tributary of the Concord River, which is itself the largest tributary of the Merrimac River.

At I, climb steeply up the far embankment, then follow the trail through the woods, with the water downhill to your right. As the trail emerges into an open area, bear right at J, then make your way back down and across the wide channel. At a junction on the far side (K), bear right. Bear right again at L, then follow the main trail as it levels and curves left. At the next trail junction after crossing a stream (M), bear right, curving right and slightly downhill into an open area. The trail becomes wide and pine-needle-carpeted, leading towards the water. At a T-junction (N) near the water's edge, detour briefly right for a fine view over the reservoir toward the Delaney Dam.

Continue left, parallel to the shore, following the main trail as trails come in from either side. Where two trails turn sharply left, take the second to continue along above the shore. The trail soon descends to water level, providing a duck's-eye view across lily pads and marsh grasses. After the trail has risen and turned away from the water, bear right at a trail junction (O). Skirt a muddy area surrounding a stream before returning to the roadside parking area.

Strange that so few ever come to the woods to see how one tree lives and grows and spires, lifting its evergreen arms to the light.
Henry David Thoreau, 1853

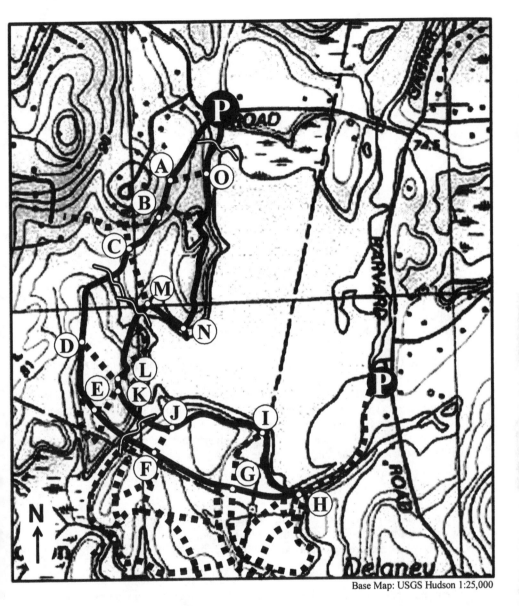

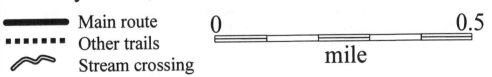

Delaney South, Harvard

——————— Main route
▪▪▪▪▪▪▪ Other trails
〜〜 Stream crossing

0   0.5
mile

19

Gardner Hill

Town: Stow
Rating: Moderate
Distance: 2.7 miles
Hiking Time: 1 - 1.5 hours
Maps: USGS Hudson / Maynard

Summary: Stow's town forest encompasses a one-time logging and mill area, gravel pits, and a stretch of the north shore of the Assabet River. A moderately challenging 2.7 mile hike takes in forest and wetland, glacial ridges along the river's edge, and the wooded summit of Gardner Hill.

Trailhead Location: From the light at the junction of 62 and 117 in Stow, drive 0.7 mile east, and turn right onto Bradley Lane. The large Town Forest parking area at the end of the lane serves nearby playing fields as well. You may also continue another 0.5 mile east on 117/62, turn right onto White Pond Road, and right again onto Heritage Lane. A parking area 0.1 mile down on the right has room for 2 cars. Follow the green-blazed trail in from the east 0.3 mile to the bridge by the start of the suggested route below.

Directions

From the Bradley Lane trailhead, enter the woods on the red-blazed trail. Pause at the footbridge over Elizabeth Brook to note the stonework along the waterway. These are remnants of the foundations of Conant's Mill, which operated here during the 19th century.

Continue across the bridge, then bear right at a Y-junction (A) to continue on the red trail. Just past a small wetland to the left, turn left onto the wide orange trail. Follow the orange trail gradually uphill past a wide intersection with the white trail. Where the yellow trail heads left, continue straight on a narrower, un-blazed trail winding through a pine glade toward a view of the Assabet River.

102

Gardner Hill, Stow

— Main route

⋯⋯⋯ Other trails

∿∿∿ Stream crossing

Base Map: USGS Hudson/Maynard 1:25,000

0   0.5

mile

N

Wintry view from bridge over Elizabeth Brook

Every winter the liquid and trembling surface of the pond, which was so sensitive to every breath, and reflected every light and shadow, becomes solid to the depth of a foot or a foot and a half, so that it will support the heaviest teams, and perchance the snow covers it to an equal depth, and it is not to be distinguished from any level field. Like the marmots in the surrounding hills, it closes its eyelids and becomes dormant for three months or more.

Henry David Thoreau (1817–1862)

At the river's edge, bear left and continue parallel to the river through a maze of interconnected paths, working your way across the hillside as the slope uphill to your left grows steeper. Climb steeply up to the top of the ridge, and bear right onto a ridge-top trail, descending again almost immediately. The trail levels and curves away from the river on a wider path. At a T-junction, turn right onto the yellow-blazed trail. The trail soon returns to the river's edge at King's Cove. Continue parallel to the river on a narrow path as the wider yellow-blazed trail bears away to the left at B (you will return here later to continue on the yellow-blazed trail). The trail soon begins a series of fairly steep up- and downhill climbs along and over a series of glacial ridges. Turn around when you please and retrace your steps to the yellow-blazed trail at B, then turn right.

Just a few minutes away from the river, take the next trail to your left and head uphill. Continue straight as another trail heads off to the right. At a T-junction, turn right and continue uphill on the un-blazed summit loop trail. The forested summit of Gardner Hill is a few minutes away. Gardner Hill is a drumlin, or till hill of clay, sand, and rocks shaped by the retreating ice. (To appreciate its shape more completely, loop left around and down the summit, rejoining your original route at the T-junction encountered on your original climb up the hill.)

To descend from the summit, take the next trail downhill to the right, and turn right onto the wider white-blazed trail. At a T-junction a few minutes ahead, turn sharply left to continue on the white-blazed trail. Bear left again when you reach the very wide blue-blazed trail. Bear right at a Y-junction (A), and downhill on the red trail to cross back over the Elizabeth Brook footbridge and return to the Bradley Lane trailhead.

Assabet River in winter from King's Cove Trail

20

Heath Hen Meadow Brook Woodland

Town: Stow
Rating: Easy
Distance: 1.4 miles
Hiking Time: 30 min. - 1 hour
Maps: USGS Hudson

Summary: This is an easy 1.4-mile tour of Heath Hen Meadow Brook and its surrounding forest and wetlands, with views over Flagg Hill Pond and neighboring Shelburne Farm Orchard. Trails are level or gently rolling, ideal for cross-country skiing in winter. Expect wet or muddy spots throughout the well-marked trail system.

Trailhead Location: From the light at the junction of Routes 62 and 117 in Stow, drive east 0.3 mile and turn right onto Packard Road. At the second stop sign, turn left onto Boxborough Road. Just after you turn, there is room to park several cars along the right (east) side of Boxborough Road.

Directions

From the kiosk on the north side of Boxborough Road, a level path with blue wooden trail markers leads to a boardwalk and railed footbridge over Heath Hen Meadow Brook. At a T-junction just on the far side of a stone fence (A), turn right, continuing on the blue trail.

Watch for the pink-blazed trail, and turn right onto it; the brook accompanies you on the right. Just before a stone fence by the edge of an orchard, the pink trail turns sharply left and runs roughly parallel to the orchard, then turns away to thread between close-growing white pines. At a trail junction, turn right, back onto the blue trail.

Continue on the blue trail past a trail junction. At a second junction in a wide clearing, detour right to climb a short but fairly steep rise to a fine view of Shelburne Farm Orchard. Return down-slope to the blue trail and turn right to continue in the same direction.

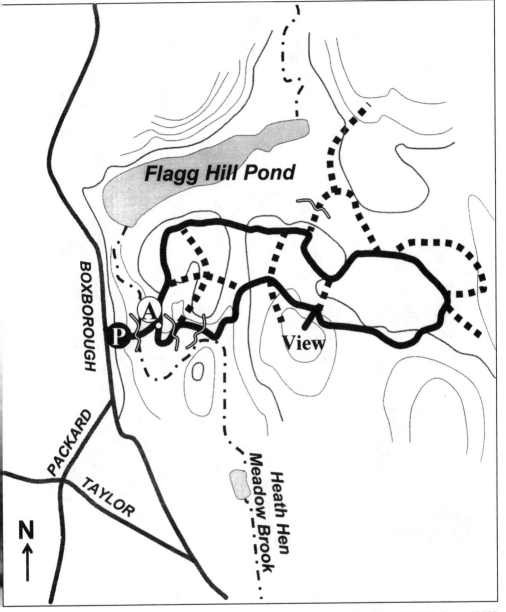

Flagg Hill Pond

BOXBOROUGH

PACKARD

TAYLOR

N

View

Heath Hen Meadow Brook

Base Map: USGS Hudson 1:25,000

Heath Hen Meadow Brook Woodland, Stow

━━━━━━ Main route
▪▪▪▪▪▪ Other trails
〜〜 Stream crossing

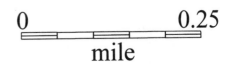

0   0.25

mile

Beaver lodge on Flagg Hill Pond

At the next junction, bear right to stay on blue. As the orchard's modern wind machines become visible, turn left on a narrow, purple-blazed trail. Where the trail meets a wide track leading to the orchard on the right, turn left and back into the forest, still on the purple trail.

The trail passes into a wetland area, with various side trails heading off to the right. At a Y-junction, bear left to continue on the purple trail. At the next junction, turn right on the wide blue-blazed trail.

Turn left at the next major junction, near the edge of Flagg Hill Pond, continuing on the blue trail through a stone fence gap and along the shore of the pond. Several other trails angle away to the left, then the blue trail curves left to run parallel to a stone fence on the right. Just before the trail curves away from the pond for good, look across the water and you may be able to spot a beaver lodge rising from the grasses. Where your trail curves right to join a path coming in from the left, you also continue to the right. As you approach a stone fence, double blue trail markers indicate that you are almost back to the entry trail. Turn right through the stone fence – junction A is easy to miss – and cross back over the footbridge and boardwalk to return to the trailhead kiosk.

Boardwalk and bridge over Heath Hen Meadow Brook

21

Heath Hen Meadow

Town: Acton
Rating: Easy
Distance: 2.8 miles
Hiking Time: 1 - 1.5 hours
Maps: Maynard

Summary: This 2.8-mile hike covers a variety of upland and wetland habitats, varying from easy strolls through meadow and forest, to rather challenging footing on the Overlook Trail as it runs alongside the Fort Pond and Heath Hen Meadow Brook wetlands. In the cold of winter, the first segment of the hike may be extended out to an island loop trail near the confluence of Muddy Brook and Heath Hen Meadow Brook.

Trailhead Location: From the junction of Routes 111 and 27 in Acton, follow 27 south for 1.1 miles, then turn right on Maple Street. After 0.6 mile, turn right onto Robbins Street. Park in the cul-de-sac at the end of Robbins.

Directions

Follow the short entrance trail to the kiosk, then continue straight on the yellow-blazed trail. At the next trail junction (A), bear left on yellow; a minute later, turn right on the blue trail.

At a T-junction by several huge white pines (B), continue straight on the red trail. The path rolls up and down on a moderately easy slope along the remnants of a glacial esker. Just past a granite outcropping, the trail descends into a wooded wetland, passable only when frozen in winter. If conditions permit, continue ahead across a stream to a small island overlooking Heath Hen Meadow Brook, flowing east from Stow's own Heath Hen conservation area.

Return to the junction of the red and blue trails, and turn left between the huge pines at B, back onto the blue trail. At a Y-junction (A) with the yellow trail, bear left to return to the kiosk, then turn left past a metal gate to continue along a meadow on the yellow trail.

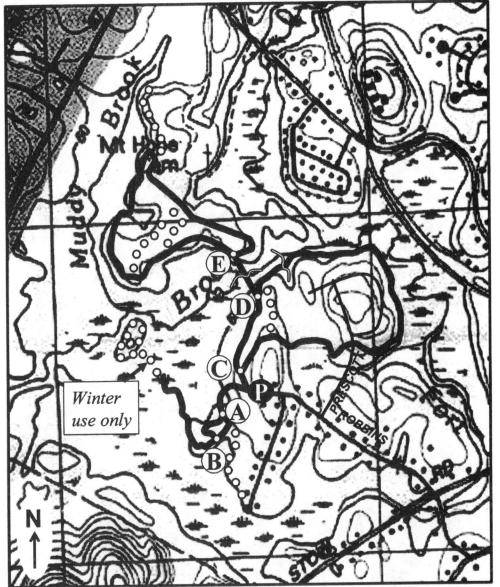

Heath Hen Meadow, Acton

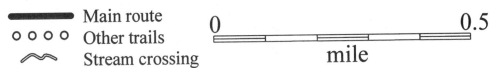

────	Main route
○ ○ ○ ○	Other trails
∿∿	Stream crossing

Base Map: USGS Maynard 1:25,000

Winter use only

0   0.5

mile

Fort Pond Brook

Bear right at C and head back into the woods on the blue trail. At a T-junction, turn right onto a red-blazed trail leading out to Prescott Road. The path crosses a wet area to a T-junction – turn left to pass through a stone fence gap to a small clearing alongside Prescott.

Cross Prescott to find a small sign for the Overlook Trail, just to the right of a private residence. Head back into the woods and over a series of footbridges crossing a wetland area. The trail angles across a stone fence, then runs parallel to the fence with the extensive wetlands of Fort Pond Brook to your right.

The narrow, uneven trail continues along the stone fence. At a point where the path widens and turns away from the wetland toward private property, turn right along the waterway and over a series of footbridges. At one spot the trail may seem to disappear underwater, and you may need to continue ahead along the top of the stone wall; the trail re-emerges shortly to the right of the fence. Follow the Overlook Trail along and then away from the wetland. At a junction with the blue trail, turn right.

At a T-junction (D), turn right and downhill; the blue trail continues left. Shortly you leave the Heath Hen property, crossing a boardwalk over Heath Hen Meadow Brook toward Mount Hope Cemetery. At a Y-junction (E) on the far side of the boardwalk, bear right. The trail rises on a steady, gentle slope. Go straight where a narrow trail heads left, then continue ahead across a wide, open area to find a narrow trail on the far side. Follow it back into the woods.

At a Y-junction, bear left. The trail curves left above the wooded wetland surrounding Muddy Brook. The trail can be moderately challenging as it angles along a slope before descending to the level of the wetland.

Pass by a trail coming in from the left, then turn left at a T-junction (you may wish to detour right briefly for a look out over the wetland. At the next Y-junction bear right, continuing to skirt the wetland to your right. A few minutes later, bear right again at E to re-cross the boardwalk and footbridge. Continue straight on yellow at D and C through forest and meadow to return to the trailhead kiosk.

> There is a pleasure in the pathless woods;
> There is a rapture on the lonely shore;
> There is society, where none intrudes,
> By the deep sea, and music in its roar:
> I love not man the less, but Nature more.
>
> Lord Byron (1788–1824)
> *Childe Harold's Pilgrimage*

Heath Hen Meadow Brook above foot-bridge

22
Grassy Pond / Nagog Hill

Town: Acton
Rating: Moderate
Distance: 3.0 miles
Hiking Time: 1 - 2 hours
Maps: USGS Billerica / Maynard

Summary: A generally easy ramble to visit Nagog and Grassy Ponds. While the 1.1-mile Grassy Pond loop is quite easy, the 1.9 mile Nagog Hill loop includes occasional moderately steep segments near the pond. The viewing platform extending out into Grassy Pond is of special interest, as is the nearby swampland boardwalk.

Trailhead Location: From the junction of Routes 2 and 27 in Acton, drive north on 27 for 1.1 miles, then turn left onto Nagog Hill Road. Drive another 1.1 miles, and you come to the Grassy Pond Conservation Area parking lot on the west side of Nagog Hill Road. The off-road lot has room for several cars. You may also park at the Nagog Hill parking lot which is a short distance south on Nagog Hill Road, on the east side of the road.

Directions – Nagog Hill Loop

From the Grassy Pond parking lot, cross Nagog Hill Road and enter the woods to the right of the Nagog Hill conservation area sign. The red-blazed trail crosses a streamlet before arriving at a junction (A on map) with the main, yellow-blazed loop trail. Continue straight, onto the yellow trail. Follow this path past two junctions with blue-blazed connector trails to the right, until you come to a Y-junction within sight of Nagog Pond. Bear left here (the yellow trail goes right), and bear left again shortly at another junction, to a T-junction near the edge of the pond. The view here extends across the water, with Littleton land to the left, and Acton ahead and to the right.

Turn right along the water's edge, cross a streamlet, and continue on parallel to the shore. As you enter a particularly dense grove of hemlocks, the trail curves to the right, away from the pond. Cross another stream on rocks, then head uphill to a trail junction below a stone fence gap. Turn right and moderately steeply uphill to a four-way junction with the yellow trail, which lies ahead and to the right. Go straight onto the yellow trail.

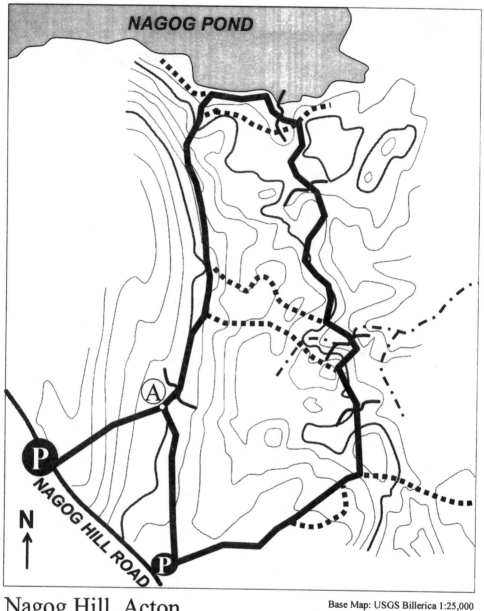

Nagog Hill, Acton

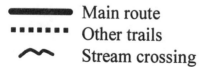

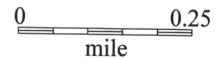

NAGOG POND

NAGOG HILL ROAD

N

Base Map: USGS Billerica 1:25,000

—— Main route
••••• Other trails
〰 Stream crossing

0   0.25
mile

Past a wetland to the right, the trail runs close by a stone fence. The fence itself may become your trail as you pass through a rather wet area. The trail rolls more steeply up and down before approaching a T-junction with the blue trail entering from the right. Turn left to continue on the yellow trail. The path soon parallels a lively flowing stream, which you cross on a wide footbridge. In winter, lovely ice formations decorate the stream's rocks and banks. The trail winds steadily uphill, curving above the stream for another minute or so before heading away into the woods.

At a T-junction at the crest of the hill, continue straight on yellow, past the second blue trail on your right, then cross a quieter stream on a footbridge. A few minutes farther along, a blue trail curves left, while the yellow trail bears right – choose either one; they converge after a few more minutes by a large pile of rocks. The trail is now wide and level.

Cross a meadow past a horse corral, then re-enter the woods. Just before the kiosk at the Nagog Hill parking area, take a sharp right to continue on the yellow loop. Pass through a small clearing, then cross a boardwalk over the wetlands surrounding a small stream. You soon arrive back at junction A. Bear left and cross Nagog Hill Road to return to the Grassy Pond parking area.

Grassy Pond viewing platform

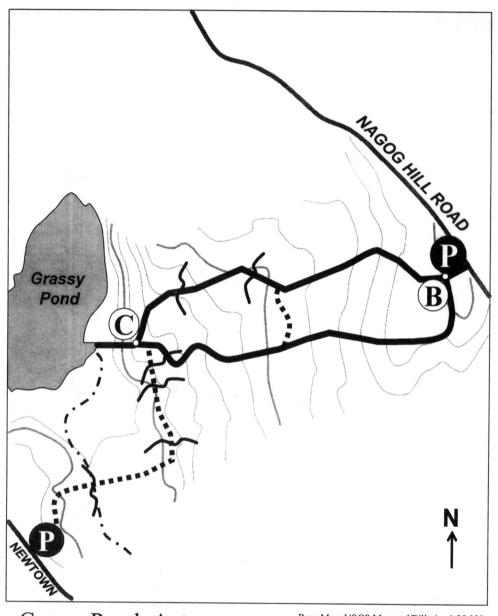

Grassy Pond, Acton

— Main route
▪▪▪▪▪▪ Other trails
〰 Stream crossing

Base Map: USGS Maynard/Billerica 1:25,000

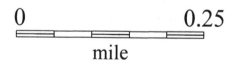

0   0.25

mile

Directions – Grassy Pond Loop

From the Grassy Pond parking area, walk directly away from Nagog Hill Road to a kiosk by junction B on map; continue straight on into the woods on the yellow loop trail. The path takes you on a steady gentle downhill route. Stay on the yellow trail when a blue-blazed connector trail leads left toward Willis Holden Drive. A boardwalk just past this trail junction carries you across a stream; pick your way over rocks to negotiate a second stream crossing a few minutes later.

You will soon see Grassy Pond emerge through the trees. At a T-junction (C), turn right. A secluded viewing platform lies just ahead across a boardwalk – a lovely place for a rest break. A great blue heron frequents this area – step quietly in case it's nearby.

When you return to junction C, continue straight on the yellow loop trail; a red trail leads right to another entrance point on Newtown Road. (You may wish to extend your hike a third of a mile out on the red trail to the long swamp boardwalk, another fascinating observation opportunity.) You soon cross two streams in quick succession; the trail then turns sharply left to run between a stone fence line to your right and the stream you just crossed.

Keep a sharp eye out for the yellow trail blazes in this area. They will lead you past a tiny, lovely pool framed by rocks, then by a larger vernal pool to the right of the trail. The path then weaves through a dense thicket of hemlock.

In a few more minutes, you arrive back at the far side of the meadow from which you started. Turn left along the near edge of the field toward the kiosk, then turn right at B to return to the parking area.

Hiking can be a pleasure any time of year. Each season has its wonders and accompanying challenges. Spring's abundant growth restores long-dormant beauty; mosquitoes, ticks and poison ivy also emerge from latency. The full flowering of summer brings heat and humidity as well, though the woods provide welcome relief. As green turns to the scarlet and gold of fall, temperatures cool and the loss of leaves opens up views that had been hidden for months. My personal favorite is winter. Despite the difficulties posed by snow-smothered or ice-crusted trails, the clean beauty and solitude of woods in winter offers a unique magnificence.

- Notes from author's journal

Beaver patrolling Nagog Pond

My mission that day was to photograph, but my expectations were low as I approached the pond -- the morning sun had disappeared behind a layer of clouds, and the light had dimmed considerably. I stepped up onto a huge fallen tree trunk to take stock and simultaneously heard an enormous splash to my left. What the...? Moments later, a small nose popped up a few yards away in the water, and the creature began looping and curving around, keeping a wary eye on me. As it passed nearby I spotted the giveaway clue: a broad, flat tail – which the beaver promptly slapped again, disappearing from view.

- Notes from author's journal

23

Nashoba Pond

Town: Westford
Rating: Moderate
Distance: 1.9 miles
Hiking Time: 45 min. - 1 hour
Maps: USGS Billerica

Summary: An easy 1.9 mile hike to a gem of a pond, the route takes you along a small glacial ridge, then around the thankfully undeveloped shores of Nashoba Pond. Horseback riders frequent the area, as do various water birds. You might hear a great horned owl hooting from the surrounding woods at dusk.

Trailhead Location: From the junction of Route 225 (Carlisle Road) and Route 27 (Acton Road) in southeastern Westford, drive west on 225. Turn left after one mile onto Texas Road. Continue to the end of the road, and park in the turn-around by the entrance to Sherlock Lane.

Directions

Walk past the sign for the Richard Semmet Conservation Land, on a trail that skirts a private yard before passing between a pair of boulders and into the woods. The trail initially rises gently; when it turns downhill, take a right onto a narrower trail, then immediately bear left and downhill at a Y-junction. (The right-hand trail soon rejoins your path.) Traverse a wide footbridge over gurgling Nonset Brook, then climb a briefly steep section. The blue-blazed trail then rolls easily before turning left to cross another footbridge over a swampier section of wetland. Just past the footbridge, bear left to curve along a fairly level section. Climb over a couple of low rises before mounting a ridge as you enter Audubon Sanctuary land. The trail runs along the ridgeline to a Y-junction above Nashoba Pond (A on map).

Descend to the right to circle the pond, making note of the ridge you've just left for your return trip. The trail around the pond almost always provides some muddy spots to challenge you, but it is a generally level and easy stroll. The pond sports small wooded islands and several sandy spots along the shoreline so you can enjoy the view from a variety of perspectives. Turn right at A to return the way you came. (An alternate loop is shown on the map, but is not recommended unless you are comfortable wading an unbridged stream that feeds Nashoba Brook.)

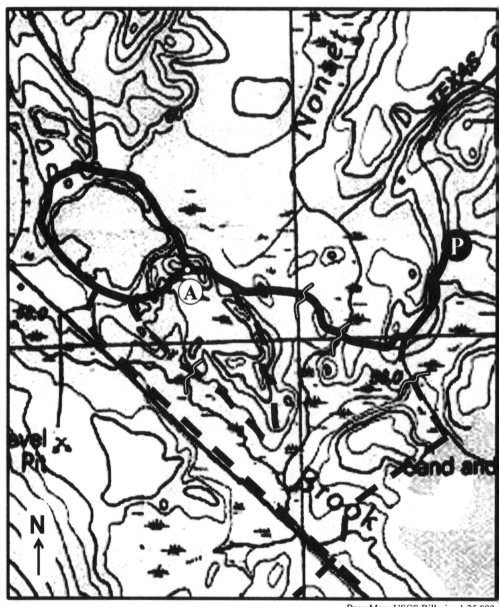

Nashoba Pond, Westford

Base Map: USGS Billerica 1:25,000

—————— Main route
– – – – Other trails
〰〰 Stream crossing

0   0.5
mile

Island in Nashoba Pond

facing page: *Confluence of Sudbury, Assabet and Concord Rivers at Egg Rock*

Concord River Watershed

24

Egg Rock

Town: Concord
Rating: Easy
Distance: 2.3 miles
Hiking Time: 45 min. - 1 hour
Maps: USGS Maynard

Summary: An easy 2.3-mile stroll through quiet woods and along the banks of the Assabet to its confluence with the Sudbury River, where the Concord River is born at Egg Rock. A brief side trip leads to a scenic overview of the Sudbury.

Trailhead Location: From the light at the junction of Main Street and Nashawtuc Road, 0.5 miles west of the Concord common, turn north on Nashawtuc. Bear right at a Y-junction where Nashawtuc becomes a loop road, then turn right onto Musterfield Road. At the next crossroad, turn right onto Simon Willard. The trailhead is 0.2 miles ahead on the right, as the road curves left, indicated by white Concord Land Conservation Trust trail markers. Several cars may park along the side of the road.

Directions

Two trails head into the woods from this point. Take the first, more southern trail, and follow the round white trail markers over a low hill and down-slope to a T-junction (A on map) with a wide trail. Turn right onto this path, which runs along a former railroad grade, now an AT&T right-of-way. After a quarter mile, the Assabet River curves in from your left, and you walk along its bank. At a Y-junction (B), bear left, away from the rail-bed and up to the top of a ridgeline, continuing along the riverbank.

Make your way across a muddy section. (In times of high water this may become impassible due to flooding.) The trail rises to the top of a knoll, then descends past a fire circle to the river confluence. The Assabet flows in from your left and the Sudbury from the right, creating the Concord at your feet.

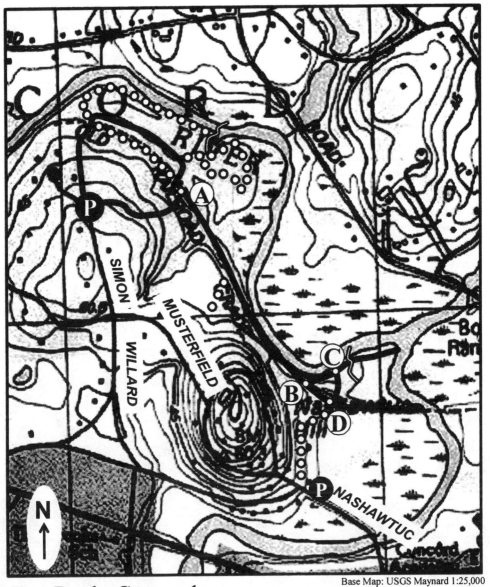

Egg Rock, Concord

▬▬▬▬	Main route
○○○○○	Other trails
∿∿∿	Stream crossing

Base Map: USGS Maynard 1:25,000

0   0.5

mile

After enjoying the scenery, return over the knoll and past the muddy spot, then bear left at a Y-junction (C). This takes you to a 4-way trail junction (D) with the rail-bed, a bit east of the point where you left it to follow the riverbank. Turn left along the railroad grade, which now juts out into the floodplain of the Sudbury. Follow it to the point where it descends to the river's edge for another scenic viewpoint. Just before the river's edge lies a small, grassy clearing – a lovely spot for a picnic.

To continue your hike, follow the railroad grade back past D, B and A – the point where you first joined it from Simon Willard Road – then take the next trail right. The narrow path descends briefly then levels before coming to a T-junction beneath the spreading boughs of a large hemlock. Turn left.

After a quarter-mile the trail curves left, and another trail branches right; continue around to the left. (The right-branching trail loops around to run along the Assabet, and would eventually connect back to this trail at the hemlock tree, except that one section is perpetually flooded.) Just ahead your trail returns to the rail-bed at a 4-way junction; continue straight, then bear right at the next junction. The gentle uphill will lead you back to Simon Willard Road just north of your starting point.

The final curves of the Sudbury River

25

Estabrook Woods

Town: Concord
Rating: Easy
Distance: 4.2 miles
Hiking Time: 1.5 - 2.5 hours
Maps: Maynard / Billerica

Summary: A 4.2-mile loop through the quiet Estabrook Woods, past ponds, swamps and glacial erratics, over streams, and through history. The heart of the woods is Harvard University's ecology study area; you'll find colonial cellar holes, a limestone quarry, and the Carlisle Minutemen's route to the old North Bridge on the eve of the American Revolution (this is the only undeveloped Minuteman route). Most trails are wide with easy footing; additional narrower trails provide further opportunities for exploration. For a really steep challenge, climb Punkatasset Hill!

Trailhead Location: From Concord Center, drive 1.2 miles northwest on Lowell Road, to a four-way stop. Turn right on Barnes Hill Road, then make a sharp left onto Estabrook Road. The suggested hike below departs from roadside parking along the west side of Estabrook, south of #393, which can accommodate several cars. Other trailheads are found at the south end of Autumn Lane in Carlisle, and along Monument Street in Concord, by #873.

Directions

Walk north along Estabrook Road. At a chain gate across the road, the pavement ends; continue on the wide dirt track. After passing private roads on your left, bear right at a Y-junction (A). Continue straight as other trails branch off to either side. Where a narrow trail heads right at a Y-junction, bear left on the main track.

At a T-junction, bear right, then right again a few minutes later at a T-junction by Hutchins Pond. The path takes you between the pond and Punkatasset Hill to your right, rising to over 300 feet in elevation. (*Optional:* A loop trail leads up the steep face of the hill and across its wooded summit before descending more gently down the northern slope; bear right to rejoin the main route.)

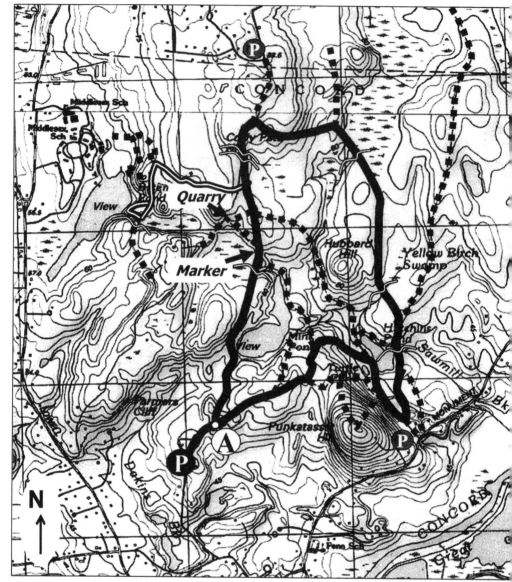

Estabrook Woods, Concord

———	Main route
===	Bateman's Pond spur
▪▪▪▪▪	Other trails
∼∼∼	Stream crossing

Base Map: USGS Maynard/Billerica 1:25,000

0   0.5
mile

Continue past the hill to a gate and kiosk by the Monument Street entrance to the Punkatasset Hill area; turn sharply left around the kiosk. The trail runs along a fence line, past open fields and pasture, then along the eastern shore of Hutchins Pond. Bear right at a Y-junction just past the pond. You are now on the Two Rod Road path, so named because of its original width. At another Y-junction about one-tenth of a mile further along, bear left.

The next mile or so of trail arcs through the Yellow Birch Swamp. After the trail passes over a stream draining the swamp, bear left at a trail junction. The next intersection, atop Cotty Pate Hill, is with the wide Estabrook Road path; turn left again. This is the route that Carlisle Minutemen took to the old North Bridge on April 19, 1775.

Estabrook Road takes you over two streams. At the next trail branching to your right, you have the option of taking a 1.3-mile round trip spur to an expansive view over Bateman's Pond.

Bateman's Pond Spur

Turn right onto the path leading uphill between two parallel lines of stone fence, watching for old cellar holes scattered throughout this area. At a Y-junction, take either branch, as they re-join shortly. At a T-junction where a faint trail heads to the right (and peters out), go left. Soon your trail meets another wide trail at a Y-junction; turn left. Wood thrush and hermit thrush song may accompany you in this area.

Pass by the first, faint trail to the right, and take the second right at a four-way junction. This trail leads to a rocky outcrop overlooking Bateman's Pond. After enjoying this first view, bear left and downhill, then straight as another trail goes sharply downhill to your right. You'll soon find a wide stone bench, placed in memory of Kevin S. Lehmann and Ross G. Hill. Have a seat and partake of another fine view across the pond.

When you are ready to continue, follow the trail leading away from the pond, parallel to a stream gurgling downhill to your right. At a T-junction, turn left and retrace your route to the Estabrook Road path.

Packed dirt and pine needles underfoot can unintentionally turn an everyday hiker into a silent wildlife scout. On the trail out to the view over Bateman's Pond, a white-tailed deer browsed through dry leaves carpeting the forest floor without noticing my approach. As she crossed the path ahead, she looked straight at me before leaping away down slope, toward the pond and out of sight. Sometimes the most unforgettable sightings are those unsought and unsuspected.
- Notes from author's journal

Bench overlooking Bateman's Pond

Oh for a seat in some poetic nook,
Just hid with trees and sparkling with a brook!

Leigh Hunt (1784–1859), *Politics and Poetics*

Continuing south on Estabrook Road, a brief detour right at the next four-way trail junction leads to a limestone quarry from colonial times. Granite fins rise from the ground, remaining from where colonists chipped out limestone. The ruins of a nearby limekiln indicate where the limestone was heated and transformed into plaster used in home and chimney construction. Return to Estabrook Road and turn right (south) on the wide track.

Just past the quarries you'll find a granite marker indicating that Concord's old North Bridge is two miles ahead. After crossing a stream that drains the swampy area to your right, the trail runs alongside Mink Pond. A ridge obscures the pond from view for a time, but soon you will find a couple of spur trails to your left that provide lovely views across the water. Shortly after the trail leaves the pond behind, you arrive back at the first junction (A) of the hike. Bear right to return to the Estabrook Road parking area.

Mink Pond

The surface of the earth is soft and impressible by the feet of men; and so with the paths which the mind travels. How worn and dusty, then, must be the highways of the world, how deep the ruts of tradition and conformity! I did not wish to take a cabin passage, but rather to go before the mast and on the deck of the world, for there I could best see the moonlight amid the mountains. I do not wish to go below now.

Henry David Thoreau, *Walden Pond*

26

Great Meadows
National Wildlife Refuge

Town: Concord
Rating: Easy
Distance: 3.1 miles
Hiking Time: 1 - 2 hours
Maps: USGS Maynard

Summary: Bring your binoculars! Wildlife is teemingly rife throughout this preserve. On a fine day in late May, local sightings included black snakes, bitterns, muskrats, great blue herons, whippoorwills, Canada geese, red-winged blackbirds, turtles, frogs, swallows and carp. The route below totals 3.1 miles, all on easy, generally wide and level paths.

Trailhead Location: Follow Route 62 east from Route 2A in Concord Center. After 1.25 miles, watch carefully for a very small *Great Meadows National Wildlife Refuge* sign on your right, and turn left onto Monson. As Monson begins to curve right, turn left into the Refuge's access road – use caution, for it is just one lane wide. Park at the second, larger lot adjacent to the observation tower if there is room.

Directions

From the main parking lot, you may first wish try your luck with binoculars from the apex of the wildlife viewing tower. Then walk past the gray gate onto the wide dirt track through the center of the refuge. Cattails fringe the vast ponds on either side; red-winged blackbirds love to perch atop them to sing their "konk-la-ree." A footbridge crosses a spillway between the two empoundments. Carp splash vigorously through the shallows. Scattered benches offer fine viewing and resting spots.

At the far end of the center trail, bear left (A on map), then head straight to the edge of the Concord River for a view of the quiet but steady flow. Continue left as the dirt track threads between pond and river, offering sweeping views to your left; the river slides invisibly by on the right behind a screen of trees. Poison ivy grows thickly along this section of trail, even encroaching on a bench, so stay to the path.

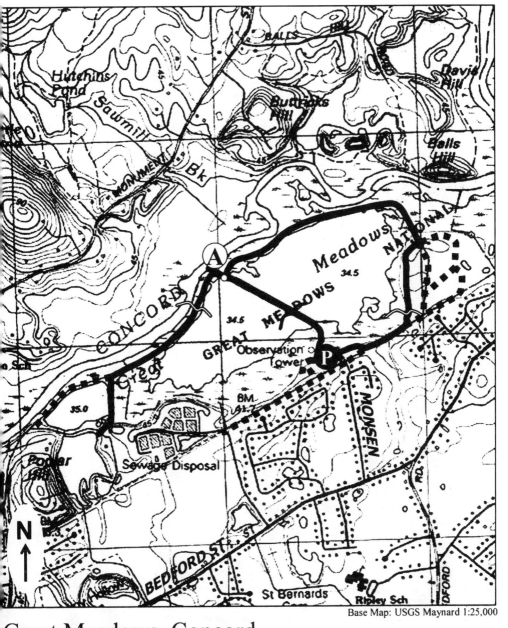

Great Meadows, Concord

▬▬▬▬	Main route
▪▪▪▪▪▪	Other trails
∿∿	Stream crossing

Base Map: USGS Maynard 1:25,000

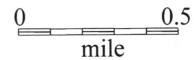

At the refuge boundary, the wide, open trail narrows as it moves into the shade of trees. Continue ahead to a trail junction at the edge of another large pond. Turn left to walk between this pond and the vast sweep of the refuge to your left. Shortly the view opens up to your right across the pond; honeysuckle and wild iris decorate its perimeter.

The trail ends a short distance ahead; retrace your steps to intersection A, and turn left to circle the eastern pond. On the far side, where the trail heads into the woods, turn right at a four-way junction, onto a narrower trail. This path leads along the pond, across a stream and up a short slope to an old railroad bed. Turn right, and continue past several benches. Watch for a narrow trail dropping back downslope to the right, and follow it back to the paved entrance road and parking lot.

> *Partway along the center trail, a whippoorwill's song exploded from the reeds to my left. I stopped to discover the bird weaving together a cluster of green stalks with a wreathing of last year's dried vegetation. After each addition, the whippoorwill emerged from the nest to perch on a nearby reed and celebrate with another energetic burst of eponymous music. What a treat to watch from just a few feet away.*
> - Notes from author's journal

The calm Concord River

27

River Meadows Reservation

Town: Carlisle
Rating: Moderate
Distance: 4.8 miles
Hiking Time: 1.5 - 3 hours
Maps: USGS Billerica

Summary: 4.8 miles of hiking through a 600-acre reservation over easy terrain, including glorious vistas over Greenough Pond and the Concord River, as well as diverse habitats from low-lying wetlands to pine forest uplands. The Concord River portion of the trail is only passable in dry seasons, and contains some wet spots even then.

Trailhead Location: From Route 225 in Carlisle center, turn northeast onto East Street. Parking for the Greenough property lies just east of the junction of East and Maple Streets in Carlisle, two miles northeast of 225, on the south side of the road. The off-road lot has space for several cars.

Directions

From the far left corner of the parking area, head into the woods, bearing left as a trail comes in from the right. The pine needle-carpeted trail winds gently downhill, arriving at a T-junction about ten minutes into the hike. Turn left towards the pond; the trail to the right leads to Maple Street.

At a Y-junction near the edge of the pond, you will turn left to stay on the main trail, but first, detour briefly right. This short spur leads to a lovely view to the left over Greenough Pond, to a large barn managed by the local Conservation Commission, and to the right up a narrow arm of the pond toward Pages Brook, feeding in from the southwest.

Continue on the main trail into the Billerica section of the reservation. After crossing a railed footbridge, turn right to continue along the pond's edge. You'll soon pass by a granite stele marking the Carlisle-Billerica town line as you re-enter Carlisle.

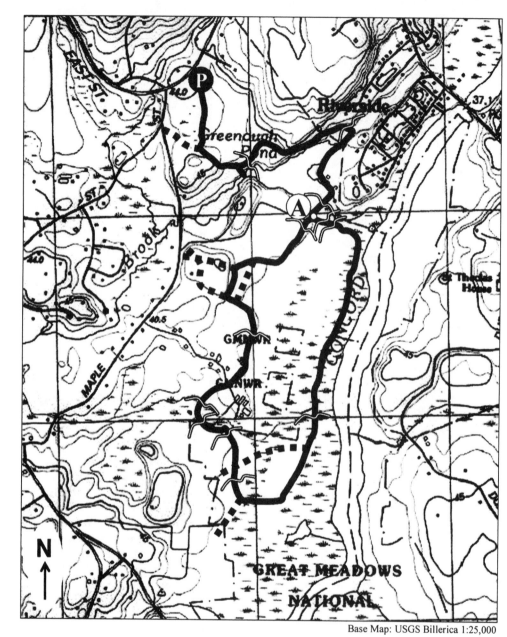

River Meadows Reservation, Carlisle

▬▬▬▬	Main route
▪▪▪▪▪▪▪	Other trails
∿∿	Stream crossing

Base Map: USGS Billerica 1:25,000

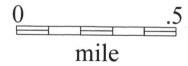

0   .5

mile

The trail emerges from the woods in front of the large white barn you may have seen earlier from across the pond. Turn right onto a dirt road along the edge of the pond, passing over spillways where the pond drains toward the Concord River about a quarter-mile to the east. As the dirt road bends to the right, follow the trail signs off the road to the left. Assuming you are hiking in the dry season, continue straight on the River Trail at A. (Alternatively, turn right toward Foss Farm for an out-and-back hike in wetter times.)

Follow the blue hiker medallions over a series of footbridges, then turn right at a trail sign by the edge of the Concord River.

A few minutes later, enter the Great Meadows National Wildlife Refuge, managed by the US Fish and Wildlife Service. Here the blue medallions are replaced by yellow USF&WS blazes. Even in the dry season, you will need to pick your way carefully across several wet spots in the next twenty minutes of hiking.

Soon after crossing a small footbridge, you reach the junction of the River Trail and the Red-Tailed Hawk Trail, which continues straight; a path to the left leads to Foss Farm, a 55-acre multi-use conservation area you may also wish to explore.

Following the Red-Tail Trail, still marked by yellow blazes, you cross two footbridges, and then go straight at a trail junction toward O'Rourke Farm and Greenough; a connector to the River Trail leads off to the right. You will cross several more small footbridges and a longer boardwalk to arrive at a trail junction marked by a USF&W regulations sign. Continue straight past the sign to wind across a vast field. After crossing a culverted stream, you leave the NWR to return to Carlisle Conservation Land and its blue hiker medallions.

At a junction with the Pine Loop Trail, bear right; turn right again at the next T-junction across a field and back into the woods. After crossing two more footbridges, you return to junction A. Turn left and then right along the dirt road. You will return the way you came, past the white barn and around Greenough Pond to the parking area.

Page's Brook, a Greenough Pond tributary

28

Great Brook Farm State Park

Town: Carlisle
Rating: Moderate
Distance: 4.1 miles
Hiking Time: 1.5 -2.5 hours
Maps: USGS Billerica

Summary: A 4.1-mile hike across widely varied terrain in the vicinity of Meadow Pond. A moderately easy 2.2-mile loop around the pond includes shoreline, woods, stream crossings and a ramble among boulders. The Heartbreak Ridge and Tophet Loop add a slightly more challenging 1.9 miles of ridge walking and swamp-skirting. Many more State Park trails lie to the north and west.

Trailhead Location: From Route 225 in Carlisle center, drive north on Lowell Road. After 1.8 miles, turn right onto Curve Street, which becomes North Road. A large off-road parking area is located on the north side of the street, 0.3 mile east of Lowell Road. Stop here and purchase a parking permit from the machine, then drive another half mile to one of two parking areas on the south side of the street, by a bridge over a stream. Note that these parking areas are closed in winter, when the only parking is at the ski touring center on Lowell Road just north of North Street.

Directions

From the parking lot, head into the woods on the Pine Pond Loop trail, along the eastern shore of the pond. A short distance along, turn right onto the Beaver Loop. The trail immediately climbs to a view over the pond, then twists and turns narrowly, with some moderate uphill and downhill climbs, above the edge of the pond. The trail passes by huge granite boulders; you can scramble up one to the right of the trail at the pond's edge for an even better view than before. Another fine viewpoint appears on a point by a picnic table; this is also your landmark for a sharp left turn as the trail levels out and heads away from the pond, back to the Pine Pond Loop.

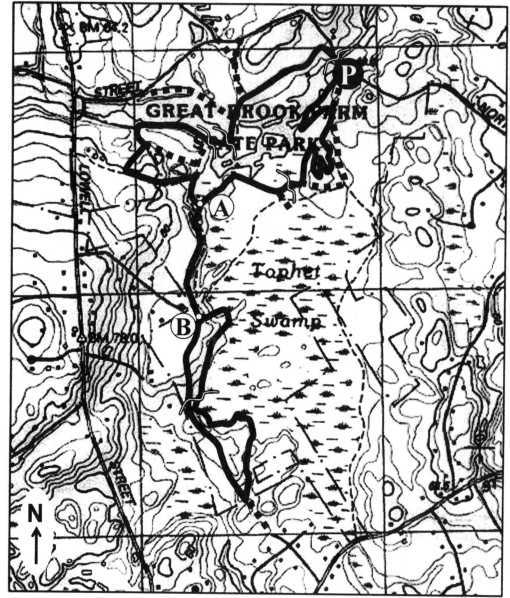

Base Map: USGS Billerica 1:25,000

Great Brook Farm State Park, Carlisle

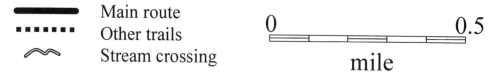

———	Main route
▪▪▪▪▪▪	Other trails
∼	Stream crossing

0   0.5

mile

Turn right onto the wide main trail. The Keyes Loop trail soon heads right, for a fifteen-minute twisting and turning tour over and through granite slabs and boulders, many decorated with sumptuous growths of moss, fern and lichen. The trail eventually bears left near the water's edge to return to the Pine Pond Loop. Turn right.

The wide path passes between wetlands and over one of Meadow Pond's outlet streams. Additional unmarked side trails are available for exploration; the most interesting perhaps is Heartbreak Ridge and the Tophet Loop, a signed and blazed trail appearing shortly after the main trail curves left past the base of a ridge. Turn left at the Heartbreak Ridge signpost (A on map) and follow the switchback trail to the top of a glacial esker. The path continues along the ridgeline to a junction just past a jumble of huge boulders. Bear left, then left again at B onto the Tophet Loop trail.

The trail descends along a ridgeline, then rolls up and down as it loops around pools to the right, with the expansive Tophet Swamp to the left. The trail continues to skirt the swamp, crossing over a boardwalk. Eventually the trail rises to higher and drier ground under tall pines and oaks. At a junction near an access trail from Woodbine Road, take a sharp right to continue around the loop. The trail passes by more pools and over a stream before climbing back up Heartbreak Ridge to the Tophet Loop junction at B. Continue straight, then bear right at a Y-junction by the boulder cluster to return back along the ridge, down the switchbacks, and back to the Pine Pond Loop trail at A. Turn left on the wide pathway.

A few minutes along the trail, take the second of two closely placed left turns and walk steadily uphill. Near the crest of the hill, turn right before a private property sign, and follow the blue trail markers downhill to a cultivated field. Turn left to circle the field along its border, enjoying a view over the Black Brook wetland to your left, sharply down slope from the edge of the field. At the base of the field, turn left, again on the wide Pine Pond trail.

After crossing the stream flowing to your right into Meadow Pond, bear left around a meadow, past the Maple Ridge Trail on your left, then bear right and uphill into an area of evergreens. At an X-junction, continue straight on the wide, level trail. The path passes an open area containing a variety of horse-jump fences, then bears right before a metal gate to return to the parking area.

> *In late March of a long, snowy winter, I spot a bird hovering with the tip of its beak to the trunk of a maple. Surely not a hummingbird, but what? Closer examination reveals a cedar waxwing – in fact the tree is serving as roost for a flock of several dozen. Remarkably, they remain while I indulge in several minutes' appreciation of their beauty.*
> — Notes from author's journal

Meadow Pond from the Beaver Loop Trail

29

Minnie Reid / Huckins Farm

Town: Bedford
Rating: Easy
Distance: 3.3 miles
Hiking Time: 1.5 - 2 hours
Maps: USGS Billerica

Summary: This 3.3-mile hike takes you through the Minnie Reid Conservation Area, across Mill Brook to the edge of the Concord River, then alongside White Cedar Swamp before looping back through the Huckins Farm area. The trails are easy except for the challenge of swampland on your way to a fine view over the Concord River by Two Brothers rocks.

Trailhead Location: West of Bedford center, from the junction of Routes 4 and 225, follow Route 4 (North Road) north for 1.8 miles. Bear left onto Chelmsford Road, and take an immediate left into the (currently unmarked) dirt parking area for the Minnie Reid Conservation Area. There is room for several cars.

Directions

Follow the trail past a boulder and away from the parking area, into the Minnie Reid Conservation Area. The trail passes through an open area past a round, blue trail marker numbered 8. Just past a stone fence, by marker 7 Blue, bear right at a Y-junction to walk parallel to the stone fence on your right. Pass by several side trails to your right. Just past marker 6 Blue lies a footbridge over Mill Brook.

The next section of trail passes through a swampy area and can be muddy or wet. On the far side where the trail rises and dries out a bit, turn right at a T-junction by 3 Orange.

After taking a right by a small granite post, the path emerges from the woods by a fenced-in paddock. Turn left and walk along the fence until the trail angles away from the enclosure. Bear left at the next Y-intersection, then left again past 5 Orange onto a dirt drive. You soon reach Dudley Road at #231; turn left along the pavement. Just before Emery Road, cross to a chain gate on the west side of Dudley. Follow the trail as it curves into the woods by 7 Orange. At a T-junction by a tennis court, turn left, following a line of utility poles.

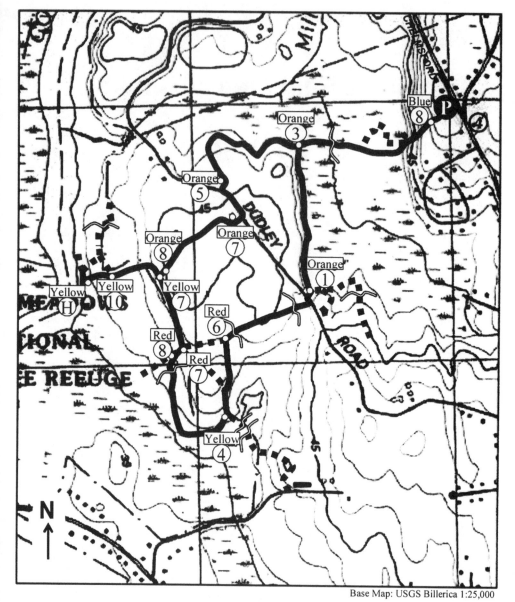

Base Map: USGS Billerica 1:25,000

Minnie Reid / Huckins Farm, Bedford

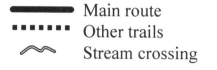

Main route

Other trails

Stream crossing

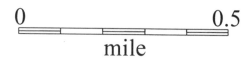

0   0.5

mile

After another quarter mile, just past marker 8 Orange, you arrive at a T-junction by the boundary of the Great Meadows National Wildlife Refuge. Turn right. Bear left at the next junction, by 10 Yellow; the Concord River lies just ahead, past a clearing marked H Yellow. Just to your right, at the river's edge are the Two Brothers rocks, where in 1638, Massachusetts Bay Colony Governor John Winthrop journeyed to mark off boundaries. The nearer rock is inscribed *Winthrop 1638*, the far one *Dudley 1638* – nearly 4 centuries of history!

After enjoying the wide-ranging river views, retrace your steps to the junction near 8 Orange; you'll now see marker 7 Yellow to your right on this side of the junction. Continue straight, along the Refuge boundary. The trail now follows along the Refuge boundary for 0.2 mile. At a 4-way intersection, turn right past 7 Red, then bear left at a Y-junction (8 Red) just ahead. This loop takes you deeper into the Refuge, where the White Cedar Swamp drains into the Concord.

As the trail turns eastward, you come to a T-junction; a small pond lies off to the right. Turn left toward the 4 Yellow marker. Bear right at the next Y-junction, by an enormous, multi-trunked pine, and continue to a T-junction by 6 Red. Turn right and follow this old cart path straight through a couple of intersections as you pass by the fields of the Huckins Farm Conservation Restriction on your way back to Dudley Road. Angle slightly left across the road and re-enter the woods by a streetlight, then turn left at 1 Orange. Your way may be occasionally wet as you skirt the swamp going back to marker 3 Orange. Turn right to re-cross Mill Brook and return to the parking area.

Concord River from Two Brothers rocks

30

Vietnam Veterans Park Ralph Hill Wood Lot

Town: Billerica
Rating: Moderate
Distance: 2.0 miles
Hiking Time: 45 min. - 1 hour
Maps: USGS Billerica

Summary: A 2-mile loop through glacier-molded woodland drops you down to the banks of the Concord River, then climbs to a 300-foot summit high above the waterway. Generally moderate, but includes one moderately steep section.

Trailhead Location: Head south from Route 3 on Treble Cove Road. After 0.4 mile, turn left into a small rotary at Vietnam Veterans Park, then immediately bear right and downhill to a large parking area on the east side of Winning Pond.

Directions

From the right side of the kiosk at the parking area walk along a paved road, past a yellow metal gate and over a spillway between Winning Pond to your right and a swampy area on the left. Follow the road as it curves left, changing to gravel and dirt as it passes between a large fenced-in area of athletic fields and a playground. Continue past another fenced enclosure (a dirt-bike track), then watch for an open area to the right of the trail, studded with boulders and a small pond. Just past the pond, turn right and step over a line of boulders to the trail.

The path climbs to the top of a small ridge and heads south. After passing over a tiny stream, which drains a small pond to the right of the trail, you scale another small ridge and then arrive at a trail junction. Turn left. The trail is level at first, but soon climbs steeply. As you crest this ridge, you catch your first glimpse of the Concord River, flowing north toward the Merrimack. While you walk, imagine the glacial forces that carved these ridges long ago.

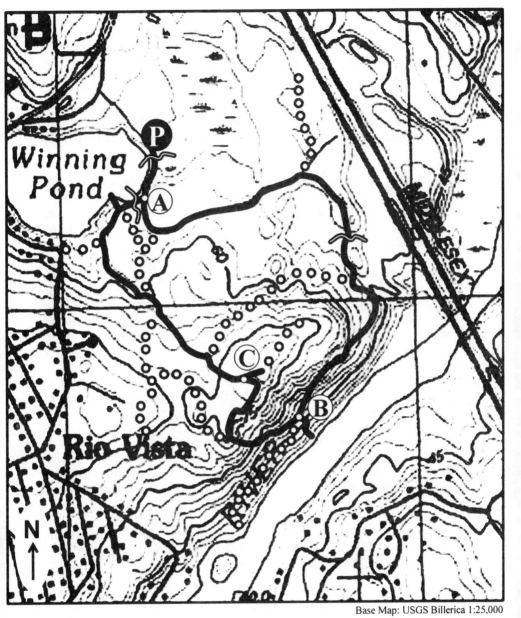

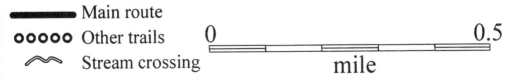

Base Map: USGS Billerica 1:25,000

Vietnam Veterans Park / Ralph Hill Woodlot, Billerica

━━━━ Main route

ooooo Other trails

〜 Stream crossing

0   0.5

mile

The path runs high above and parallel to the river, rising and falling through oak and pine. The land continues to rise to the right of the trail, with occasional granite outcroppings and many boulders decorating the slope

The first Sudbury Valley Trustees boundary marker appears as the trail begins a gentle descent, angling closer to the river. You shortly arrive at a Y-junction (B) facing a rocky outcropping that overlooks the river beyond. This is a nice spot to descend to the river's edge for a break. To do so, take the trail to the left around the outcrop.

After enjoying the riverside view, return to B, and head uphill (avoiding another trail to the left parallel to the river), angling across the slope and away from the river on a moderately steep grade. The trail grows steeper, winding among boulders. The slope eases as houses become visible to the left of the trail. Watch for a large orange-painted blaze, and turn right at the T-junction.

The trail now rolls easily uphill among an area of knolls, passing a closed section of trail before arriving at a T-junction (C). Your route continues left at this point; first, detour right to ascend to the 300-foot summit you have been circling. The river is not visible, but the sense of altitude is palpable as the ground drops away steeply to the southeast. Several nearby rocks make handy seats if another rest break is in order after the climb.

Return down the main trail past C, bearing right where a trail to the left is marked as closed. At the next T-junction, turn left, continuing downhill. The path is edged with fallen tree trunks as it curves through oak and pine.

Turn right at the next junction, toward an orange-diamond marker, then left at the following intersection a short distance along. This trail segment curves right to run near the shore of Winning Pond. At an open, pine-needle-carpeted glade, detour left to gaze out over the lake. You may see Canada geese cruising about, honking to their mates.

Continue ahead to a Y-junction, and bear left. The trail dips to cross a small stream, then rises into the open area near the playground and ball fields (A). Walk straight along the paved road to return to the parking area.

Winning Pond

Glossary of Terms

Drumlin: A streamlined hill or ridge of glacial drift with its long axis paralleling the direction of flow of the former glacier.

Erratic: Large water-worn boulders transported by glacier ice, different from the bedrock on which it lies.

Esker: Serpentine ridges of gravel and sand, taken to mark channels in the decaying ice sheet, through which streams washed much of the finer drift, leaving the coarser gravel between the ice walls.

Glacial Drift: Sediment deposited by bodies of glacial melt-water.

Kame: A low, steep-sided hill of stratified drift, formed in contact with glacial ice. (Scottish term)

Kettle, kettlehole: A depression in drift, made by the wasting away of a detached mass of glacier ice that had been wholly or partly buried in the drift.

Stele: A usually carved or inscribed stone slab or pillar.

Trailside Pond

Additional Resources

Regional Groups

Assabet River Rail Trail
    246 Essex Street
    Marlborough MA 01752
    http://www.arrtinc.org/

Bay Circuit Alliance (Bay Circuit Trail)
    3 Railroad Street
    Andover, MA 01810
    http://www.serve.com/baycircuit/

Friends of the Assabet River NWR
    P.O. Box 5729
    Marlboro, MA 01752-8729
    http://www.farnwr.org/index.html

Massachusetts Audubon Society
    208 South Great Road
    Lincoln MA 01773
    http://www.massaudubon.org/

Massachusetts State Parks (trail maps)
    251 Causeway Street, Suite 600
    Boston MA 02114
    http://www.state.ma.us/dem/parks/trails.htm

Organization for the Assabet River (OAR)
    Damonmill Square
    Concord MA 01742
    http://www.assabetriver.org/about.html

SuAsCo Watershed (MA Exec. Office of Environmental Affairs)
    180 Beaman Street
    West Boylston MA 01583
    http://www.state.ma.us/envir/mwi/suasco.htm

Sudbury Valley Trustees
    18 Wolbach Road, Sudbury MA 01776
    978-443-5588
    http://sudburyvalleytrustees.org/

The Trustees of Reservations
    Long Hill, 572 Essex Street
    Beverly MA 01915
    http://www.thetrustees.org/

Trail Guides and Maps
Listed Alphabetically by Town

Acton	Conservation Department, Town Hall, 472 Main Street, Acton MA 01720 (978) 264-9631	Book $10
Bedford	Bedford Conservation Commission, 10 Mudge Way, Bedford, MA 01730 (781) 275-6211	Maps - No charge
Bolton	Town Clerk, Town Hall, 663 Main Street, Bolton MA 01740 (978) 779-2771	Book $10
Carlisle	Town Clerk, Town Hall, 66 Westford St, Carlisle, MA 01741 (978) 369-6155	Book $5
Concord	Concord Natural Resources and Conservation, 141 Keyes Road, Concord MA 01742 (978) 318-3285	Map $10
Harvard	Harvard Conservation Trust, PO Box 31, Harvard, MA 01451 (978) 456-3552	Book $10
Northborough	Engineering Department, Town Hall, 63 Main Street, Northborough 01532 (508) 393-5015	Maps - No charge
Southborough	Recreation Department, 17 Common Street, Southborough MA 01772 (508) 485-0710	Maps - No charge
Stow	Conservation Commission, Town Hall, 380 Great Road, Stow MA 01775 (978) 897-4514	Book $10
Wayland	Wayland Public Library, 5 Concord Rd, Wayland, MA 01778-1901 (508) 358-2311	Maps $0.10 each
Westford	Roudenbush Community Center, 65 Main Street, Westford, MA 01886 (978) 692-5511	Book $4

Website URLs
arranged alphabetically by Town

Acton   **Acton Conservation Lands**
http://www.town.acton.ma.us/LSCOM/index.htm

Ashland   **Ashland State Park**
http://www.state.ma.us/dem/parks/ashl.htm

Bedford   **Town-Owned Conservation Areas**
http://www.town.bedford.ma.us/conservation/cons_areas.html

Berlin   **Garfield Woods (SVT)**
http://www.sudburyvalleytrustees.org/Visit/Sites/Garfield.html

---

Bolton   **Bolton Conservation Trust**
http://www.boltonconservationtrust.org/

Boxborough   **Boxborough Conservation Lands**
*http://www.town.boxborough.ma.us/boxborough/cgi-
bin/makepage.cgi?map=map_consland.html*

Carlisle   **Carlisle Conservation and Recreation Areas**
http://www.carlisle.org/ (Click on "Conservation")

Great Brook Farm State Park
http://www.state.ma.us/dem/parks/gbfm.htm

Concord   **Conservation Land Guide**
http://www.concordnet.org/dplm/Land%20Guide.html

Estabrook Woods
http://www.walden.org/scholarship/e/ells_steve/estabrook/

Walden Pond
http://www.state.ma.us/dem/parks/wldn.htm

White Pond
http://www.whitepond.org/

Framingham	**Callahan State Park** *http://www.state.ma.us/dem/parks/call.htm* **Wayside Inn Road Properties (SVT)** *http://www.sudburyvalleytrustees.org/Visit/Sites/WaysideInn.html* **Welch Reservation (SVT)** *http://www.sudburyvalleytrustees.org/Visit/Sites/Welch.html*
Harvard	**Harvard Conservation Trust** *http://www.brightleaf.com/hct/*
Hopkinton	**College Rock** *http://www.hopkinton.org/government/conservation/college.htm* **Hopkinton Area Land Trust** *http://www.hopkinton.org/community/groups/halt.htm* **Hopkinton State Park** *http://www.state.ma.us/dem/parks/hpsp.htm* **Waseeka Wildlife Sanctuary (Audubon)** *http://www.massaudubon.org/Nature_Connection/Sanctuaries/unstaffed_sanct/waseeka.html* **Whitehall State Park** *http://www.state.ma.us/dem/parks/whit.htm*
Lincoln	**Lincoln Conservation Commission** *http://www.lincolntown.org/conserve.htm* **Drumlin Farm (Audubon)** *http://www.massaudubon.org/Nature_Connection/Sanctuaries/Drumlin_Farm/index.html* **Lincoln Land Conservation Trust** *http://www.lincoln-ma.com/town_groups/llct.htm*
Littleton	**Littleton Conservation Trust** *http://littletonconservationtrust.org/guide/index.html*
Maynard	**Maynard Conservation Commission Trails** *http://web.maynard.ma.us/gov/conscom/trails/*

Natick	**Broadmoor Wildlife Sanctuary (Audubon)** *http://www.massaudubon.org/Nature_Connection/* *Sanctuaries/Broadmoor/index.html* **Cochituate State Park** *http://www.state.ma.us/dem/parks/coch.htm* **Natick Conservation Commission** *http://www.infotech-* *maine.com/natickma/commdev_website/pages/ncc.html* **Natick Town Forest** *http://home.att.net/~SalsTrails/summer/natdoc.htm*
Northborough	**Northborough Parks and Recreation** *http://www.town.northborough.ma.us/town%20departments/* *recreation/web%20page%20rec.htm*
Southborough	**Southborough Open Land Foundation** *http://www.solf.org/properties.html* **Turenne Wildlife Habitat (SVT)** *http://www.sudburyvalleytrustees.org/Visit/Sites/Turenne.html*
Stow	**Stow Conservation Trust** *http://www.stowconservationtrust.org/*
Sudbury	**Brues Woods (SVT)** *http://www.sudburyvalleytrustees.org/Visit/Sites/BruesWoods.html* **Sudbury Conservation Lands** *http://home.att.net/~sudbury.concom/conserva.htm* **Gray Reservation (SVT)** *http://www.sudburyvalleytrustees.org/* *Visit/Sites/GrayReservation.html* **Lyons-Cutler Reservation (SVT)** *http://www.sudburyvalleytrustees.org/Visit/Sites/Lyons.html* **Round Hill (SVT)** *http://www.sudburyvalleytrustees.org/Visit/Sites/RoundHill.html*

Wayland	**Wayland Conservation Areas**
	http://www.wayland.ma.us/conservation/ConservationAreaPage.htm

Cow Common
http://home.att.net/~salstrailsmaps/cwmdw.gif

Hamlen Woods (SVT)
http://www.sudburyvalleytrustees.org/
Visit/Sites/HamlenWoods.html

Sedge Meadow (SVT)
http://home.att.net/~salstrailsmaps/sedge.gif

Upper Mill Brook (SVT)
http://www.sudburyvalleytrustees.org/
Visit/Sites/UpperMillBrook.html

Westborough   **Westborough Hiking Areas**
http://www.westboroughcharm.org/guide/index.htm

Walkup and Robinson Memorial Reservation (SVT)
http://www.sudburyvalleytrustees.org/
Visit/Sites/WalkupRobinson.html

Westford   **Westford Conservation Trust**
http://www.westfordconservationtrust.org/ (Click on "Trails")

Nashoba Brook Wildlife Sanctuary (Audubon)
http://www.massaudubon.org/Nature_Connection/
Sanctuaries/unstaffed_sanct/nashoba_brook.html

Weston   **Jericho Forest**
http://www.westonlandtrust.org/newsletter/index.html

Trail Guides   *http://westonforesttrail.org/guides/*

Trail Maps   *http://westonforesttrail.org/walks/maps/*

Weston Forest and Trail Association
http://westonforesttrail.org/

Weston Land Trust   *http://www.westonlandtrust.org/*

Author's Website containing all the above links:
http://home.comcast.net/~hikesuasco/wsb/html/view.cgi-resources.html-.html

---

Also Available from
New England Cartographics

Maps

Holyoke Range State Park (Eastern Section)	$3.95
Holyoke Range/Skinner State Park (Western Section)	$3.95
Mt. Greylock Reservation Trail Map	$3.95
Mt. Toby Reservation Trail Map	$3.95
Mt. Tom Reservation Trail Map	$3.95
Mt. Wachusett & Leominster State Forest Trail Map	$3.95
Western Massachusetts Trail Map Pack (all 6 above)	$15.95
Quabbin Reservation Guide	$4.95
Quabbin Reservation Guide (waterproof version)	$5.95
Grand Monadnock Trail Map	$3.95
Wapack Trail Map	$3.95
Connecticut River Recreation Map (in Massachusetts)	$5.95

Books

Guide to the Metacomet-Monadnock Trail	$12.95
Hiking the Pioneer Valley	$14.95
Hiking the Monadnock Region	$12.95
High Peaks of the Northeast	$12.95
Great Rail Trails of New Jersey	$16.95
Skiing the Pioneer Valley	$10.95
Golfing in New England	$16.95
Bicycling the Pioneer Valley	$10.95
Steep Creeks of New England	$14.95
Hiking Green Mountain National Forest (Southern Section)	$14.95
Birding Western Massachusetts	$16.95
Waterfalls of Massachusetts	$14.95

Please include postage/handling:

$0.75 for the first map and $0.25 for each additional map;
$1.50 for the Western Mass. Map Pack;
$2.00 for the first book and $1.00 for each additional book.

Postage/Handling _____

Total Enclosed _____

(Order Form is on next page)

*Ask about our GEOLOPES -- stationery and envelopes made out of recycled USGS topographic maps. Free samples available upon request.

ORDER FORM

To order products, call or write:

New England Cartographics
     P.O. Box 9369
     North Amherst MA 01059
     (413) - 549-4124
     FAX orders: (413) - 549-3621
     www.necartographics.com

Circle one of the following:

Mastercard   Visa   AMEX   Check   Money Order

Card Number _____

Expiration Date _____

Signature _____

Telephone (optional) _____

Please send my order to:

Name _____

Address _____

Town/City _____

State _____ **Zip** _____

Visit our web site
www.necartographics.com

160